GW00758892

STEWART PARKER
DRAMATIS PERSONAE
& OTHER WRITINGS

edited by
Gerald Dawe
Maria Johnston
Clare Wallace

Litteraria Pragensia
Prague 2008

Published 2008 by Litteraria Pragensia
an imprint of Charles University
Faculty of Philosophy
Náměstí Jana Palacha 2, 116 38 Prague 1
Czech Republic
www.litterariapragensia.com

The publication of this book has been supported by research grant
MSM0021620824 "Foundations of the Modern World as Reflected in Literature
and Philosophy" awarded to the Faculty of Philosophy, Charles University,
Prague, by the Czech Ministry of Education.

Cataloguing in Publication Data

Stewart Parker: Dramatis Personae & Other Writings; edited by Gerald Dawe,
Maria Johnston and Clare Wallace.—1st ed.
      p. cm.
     ISBN 978-80-7308-241-3 (pb)
     1. Modern Drama. 2. Irish Studies. 3. Irish Literature.
     I. Parker, Stewart. II. Gerald Dawe. III. Title

Printed in the Czech Republic by PB Tisk
Typeset and design by lazarus

Stewart Parker was born in Belfast in 1941. A member of a group of young writers which included Seamus Heaney and Bernard Mac Laverty in the early sixties at Queen's University, he went on to graduate with an MA in poetic drama and then taught at Hamilton College and Cornell University. Following his return from America, he worked as a freelance writer in Belfast until 1978, contributing a column on pop music to *The Irish Times*. His radio plays include *The Iceberg* (1975) and *The Kamikaze Ground Staff Reunion Dinner* (1980). His TV plays include *I'm a Dreamer Montreal* (1979), *Iris in the Traffic, Ruby in the Rain* (1981); *Joyce in June* (1981), *Blue Money* (1984), *Radio Pictures* (1985) and *Lost Belongings* (1987). His first stage play *Spokesong* (1975) won the 1976 *Evening Standard* Most Promising Playwright Award and *I'm a Dreamer Montreal* won the Ewart-Biggs Memorial Prize. His work for the theatre includes *Catchpenny Twist* (1977), *Nightshade* (1980), *Pratt's Fall* (1983), *Northern Star* (1984), *Heavenly Bodies* (1986) and *Pentecost* (1987) which won he Harvey's Irish Theatre Award. He died in London in 1988.

Gerald Dawe is the author of *The Proper Word: Collected Criticism* (2007) and *My Mother-City* (2007), as well as six collections of poetry. He is a fellow of Trinity College Dublin and Director of the Oscar Wilde Centre for Irish Writing at the School of English TCD.

Maria Johnston recently completed a PhD at Trinity College Dublin on the poetry of Sylvia Plath and is the co-editor, with Gerald Dawe, of *High Pop: Stewart Parker's Irish Times Column*, for Lagan Press.

Clare Wallace is author of *Suspect Cultures: Narrative, Identity and Citation in 1990s New Drama* (2006) and editor of *Monologues: Theatre, Performance, Subjectivity* (2006). She is Deputy Chair of the Department of Anglophone Literatures and Cultures, at Charles University, Prague.

Acknowledgements

Dramatis Personae & Other Writings was compiled by Gerald Dawe and Maria Johnston with the assistance of Lesley Bruce, Hugh Odling-Smee and the staff of the Linen Hall Library, Belfast to whom kind acknowledgement is made. In addition, Clare Wallace would like to thank Marilynn Richtarik for supplying "Signposts" and "The Green Light/Self Portrait," and Lesley Bruce for providing the photographs for the volume. All photographs are by John Gilbert.

Research for this book has been also generously assisted by grant support from the Department of Foreign Affairs, Ireland, and the Czech Ministry of Education.

Contents

Preface

The stories and reflections in this collection of Stewart Parker's literary journalism mirror much of the tone ("the crux" as he called it) of his dramatic writing, displaying characteristically shrewd commentary and astute observation. Here James Joyce ("Stewart's passion," according to his niece, theatre director, Lynne Parker) rubs shoulders with Sam Thompson (the much neglected Belfast playwright), learning Irish in troubled Belfast shades into teaching writing in an American prison, the politics of history shape up to the power of play, and always, at the core, Parker's men and women:

> One thing [Belfast] can still glory in, and that's its women. A superior brand of dynamite. Argue about it all you like, but frankly they're more attractive than anywhere else I've ever been. It must have to do with the toughness of being a woman—and in a particularly unliberated society—allied to all the other rigours of growing up in the place. You need character to survive all that. And by God they've got it. Only a Belfast woman could have conceived the idea of a guerrilla peace campaign.

Parker is also willing to say some things about "the tenacious archaism of Irish culture," which would not have endeared him to the (betimes) self-regarding Irish literary establishment. He remained strangely a perpetual outsider, who could not, as he writes in "Buntus Belfast," "sink my identity in Dublin, nor in New York or in London or Glasgow either," even though he was such an indispensable part of the theatre scene that links together Belfast, Derry, Dublin, London, Edinburgh, Glasgow, London and Birmingham. His moving from Belfast to North America, back to Belfast, Edinburgh and London, and his ties with these and other cities and places, meant that he could not be tied down.

Again, Lynne Parker's comment is apt when she remarks that Parker "would be the first to point out that a confused, or at least, multi-layered, sense of identity was part of his psychological heritage," and an obvious source of inspiration to all that is included here. Also a sign of his honesty as he says: "On the one hand, you can't forget a nightmare while you are still dreaming it. On the other, it is survival through comprehension that is healthy, not survival through amnesia. Besides, the past is not a dead letter. The past is explosive cargo in everybody's dresser. Your grandfather is the past." While here he is puncturing another bubble—the much mythologized Sixties: "For the further those years recede, the more cheap and shallow and narcissistic and downright embarrassing they appear. Really, they were mainly remarkable for the final triumph of the admass, the victory of style over substance, of trend over conviction, of appearances over values. The seventies have been drab by contrast, defensive, uncertain, wracked by traumas. But on balance I prefer them in every way—including musically."

There is something elusive about Stewart Parker, in the same way that there is something unknown, unknowable, about the cultural matrix out of which he came, an East Belfast Protestant; or, in his own words, "Scots-Irish, Northern English, immigrant Huguenot ... in short, the usual Belfast mongrel crew."

If Belfast is the live wire that electrifies Parker's writing, ("stocious," "thick," "all the rage" buzz with Belfast street life), his heroes and heroines come from all over the shop. From the revered Joyce, to the little known radical northern educationalist, John Malone, whose memorial lecture Parker gave in June 1986, only a couple of years before his own death.

The tragic irony is that Stewart Parker was made for our present-day world. What he would have done with the epoch of MTV, the fatuous lure of "celebrity," Big Brother, the Jerry Springer Show, Reality TV, the mind-numbing banality of lifestyle magazines, tabloid truth, love islands, we can but imagine. He would have had a field day. As this collection shows Stewart Parker was a man of the world. He knew America well and had a clear-eyed view of both Ireland and Britain.

What comes across throughout these pages is Stewart Parker's anticipation and intelligence of the changing cultural conditions of theatre life and play-making in the closing decades of the twentieth century. Alongside this alert cosmopolitan sensibility, Parker's experience of living in and through Belfast's self-inflicted wounding made him keenly aware of what happens when politics fails to deliver a democratic answer to the contradictory beliefs of ordinary citizens. His innate scepticism about politics is etched herein with feisty and unambivalent vigour.

"It seems to me that a writer's personal politics are actually neither here nor there; it's only the politics embodied in and expressed through the work that matter; and the two are often interestingly at odds, for the imagination dredges far deeper than opinions or even convictions. Further, the fruits of the imagination are earned through long and arduous labour, and I see no point in selling it short with an easy recitation of banal slogans, however sincerely meant"—sound and solid good sense and good reason why *Dramatis Personae & Other Writings* is such a valuable book for today.

As he says in his tribute to Sam Thompson, "Like any true writer, it was in his work that he truly lived, and still lives." So it is fitting, given his deep-seated faith in the theatre, that *Dramatis Personae & Other Writings* concludes with articles on the theatre—and his wonderful story about the genesis and history of the television series, *Lost Belongings*, a story of perseverance if ever there was one—and upon his musing upon his background and his own plays.

Gerald Dawe

PART ONE

Dramatis Personae
John Malone Memorial Lecture

Among my souvenirs, there is the 1955 programme of a school play. The school was Ashfield Boys' Secondary and the play was the great fifteenth-century allegorical drama, *Everyman*. As to the cast-list, it reads to me now as the poignant roll-call of a Protestant East Belfast childhood: Messenger Alex McIlroy, Beggar Tommy Cranston, Good Deeds Brian Tosh, Knowledge Billy Scully, Strength John Bell, Beauty Roy Smyth—he must have suffered a bit—Death Tommy Lecompte, Everyman Stewart Parker. The producer and director was John Malone.

I was thirteen at the time. But I remember the feel of the experience with an undimmed intensity, since it constituted my introduction to the theatre, and the theatre has since become my life's work.

I have a very poor and highly selective memory. For example, I have no recollection whatsoever of John Malone's formal teaching of English during my two years at Ashfield. Along with the playing of Everyman, I have just one other vivid memory of the time, and I'm afraid it is of yet another performance. Having discovered my enthusiasm for the conjuring set I'd received as a Christmas present, John invited me to perform my magic tricks for the rest of the class. I thereby experienced for the first time that heady and highly addictive sensation of putting one over on an audience.

John Malone was an enthusiast who responded with warmth and delight to the enthusiasm of others, and in particular to those of his pupils. In his openness and sensitivity to my own blind, gawky, fledgling creative impulses, he succeeded in teaching me, at that early age, that there is a necessary and vital polarity in drama: between *Everyman* and sleight of hand, between the Four Last Things and the three card trick, between poetry and patter, art and show business. It was the first and greatest of all the many debts to him which I incurred over the years, and which makes me grateful for the opportunity to commemorate the man and his work here this evening.

It is hardly surprising that he should have started an article, published in the Spring 1973 issue of the magazine *Threshold*, with the words: "Drama is the most natural form of education." Having expatiated on this a little, he continues:

> Why, then, if it's so natural, have special pleas to be made for Drama in Education? Why is it so often regarded as an educational frill, something peripheral to the real business of education? Traditionally educational thinking has tended to be excessively intellectualist, implying that our thinking mainly proceeds through a process of abstraction and that our head rather than our whole body and being is involved in thought. No-one interested in education would want to deny the importance of abstract thought: the point is it can best develop out of a rich lived experience in which heart as well as mind, body as well as head are involved.

It is clear from this that there was nothing arbitrary about his choice of *Everyman* for Ashfield's first-ever school play. For in *Everyman* abstract thought puts on flesh and blood. The Messenger announces it to us as a Morality play, but the lesson in morality is subsumed in a story which engages directly with our feelings. God sends his mighty messenger Death to summon his renegade subject Everyman to judgement. Everyman is caught unawares, his book of account is not made up, he tries to bargain with Death, to no avail. The journey towards the final reckoning begins. Time is running out. Who will save him?

He goes first for help to his Fellowship, then to his Kindred and Cousin, then to his Goods and Riches—and is spurned and abandoned by each of them in turn. Finally he tries his Good Deeds. But she is too weak and malnourished to stand up.

The turning-point of the story is now reached in the play's best-remembered moment. Good Deeds tells Everyman:

> Though that on my feet I may not go
> I have a sister that shall with you also,
> Called Knowledge, which shall with you abide
> To help you to make that dreadful reckoning.

Whereupon Knowledge enters and says:

> Everyman, I will go with thee and be thy guide
> In thy most need to go by thy side.

There is a powerful force at work here. We can of course acknowledge with our heads the underlying meaning of the allegory—that our knowledge will point us towards salvation if we allow ourselves to be guided by it. But all this is bypassed by our far more profound emotional response as an audience to a gesture of charity and solidarity which transforms the whole human journey for us at last with a possibility of hope. It is a particular and yet a universal moment, which we encounter in many other places; as in the Old Testament, when Ruth says to her bereaved mother-in-law Naomi, as the latter prepares to depart for her homeland:

> Intreat me not to leave thee, or to return from following after thee: for whither thou goest I will go; and where thou lodgest, I will lodge; thy people shall be my people, and thy God my God.

However, it is worth remarking in passing that the dramatic force of the two lines which Knowledge speaks to Everyman lies in gesture and not just in declaration, much less in explanation. Despite the brevity and bareness of the language—or more likely because of them—the moment carries at least as much emotional power for me as Ruth's beautifully-wrought speech. Dramatic writing is gestural before it is literary; but by the same token it needs a stage or screen, an actor and an audience, fully to unfold its meaning.

But I have already digressed for in the article from which I was quoting, John Malone was less concerned with drama as a subject in itself than with role-playing and enactment, the mechanics of performance, as an educational tool. Let me quote him further:

> Viewed in this context Drama in Education is not only a subject like Maths or Geography but a means to education in virtually every subject in the curriculum and at every stage of learning.

I believe this to be incontrovertible—if for the word Drama we substitute the word Play. It appears to me that we learn nothing of consequence other than through Play. Writers in various disciplines have demonstrated how primal the impulse to play is, throughout the animal kingdom. The Dutch philosopher of history, Johan Huizinga, has established in his elegant and eloquent study, *Homo Ludens*, that civilization itself arises and unfolds in and as play. He postulates Homo Ludens, Man the Player, as at least equal in importance to those other anthropological hypotheses, Homo Sapiens, Man The Thinker and Homo Faber, Man the Maker. Ludo ergo sum: I play therefore I am. Play is how we test the world and register its realities. Play is how we experiment, imagine, invent, and move forward. Play is above all how we enjoy the earth and celebrate our life upon it.

It is no accident of etymology that this fundamental animal instinct, this self-sufficient force shaping the very evolution of human society, should share its name with those works of fiction which are presented by actors before an audience—the stage play, the screenplay, the radio and television play—these are merely particular and local forms of the play-force, consciously shaped, fashioned by human imagination and usage into a highly sophisticated kind of game, the rules of which have remained surprisingly constant for well over two thousand years, the purposes and intentions of which may vary as between societies and historical periods and artistic movements and individuals.

Although I never properly discussed the matter with John Malone, my guess is that in general he favoured drama the purpose of which was to instruct in some degree. I say this because of his inexhaustible zeal for the inculcation of sound values. In fact if I had to write a Morality play around him, I think I would probably select from amongst all the possible names with which to characterise him—Integrity, Commitment, Service, and so on—the allegorical name of Zeal. He was a true zealot for the emancipation of the mind and imagination, and for an educational system which would afford the greatest nurture to the least naturally endowed child in the most wretched environment in the land. It was a zeal which drew its force from such diverse traditions as Northern Irish Protestant radicalism, a particular brand of Christian socialism, and a Cambridge Leavisite aesthetic. It was a quietly crusading zeal which instinctively fixed on anything and everything within its ken as a potential learning resource: drama included.

But should plays actually aim to instruct? In what sense can they do so?

Everyman is unquestionably a play which aims to instruct. In a general way it cautions us to take heed, since death will strike when we are least prepared for it, and all the earthly pleasures which we hold dear will prove to be transient and useless: only a wise mind and good deeds will stand to us. More particularly, it scolds its fifteenth-century pre-Reformation flock for straying from orthodoxy and not observing the sacraments. There is even a long and rather extraneous passage which is a kind of commercial for the priesthood; although I seem to recall that John Malone prudently cut this from his production, along with the character of Confession, in deference to the theological proclivities of his Ashfield School audience.

Drama in our own time is not usually as straightforwardly didactic as that. But there is a major tradition in this century of committed socialist playwriting, with a didactic intention. Its greatest and most influential exponent has of course been Bertolt Brecht. From the point in his mid-twenties when he became a convinced Marxist, Brecht applied himself not just to developing a new theatre for the new age of scientific materialism, but a comprehensive philosophical rationale for such a theatre. For a time, both theory and practice inclined towards straightforward agitprop as in the "Lehrstücke" or "learning-play," a species of didactic cantata which he wrote in conjunction with like-minded composer friends, such as Kurt Weill and Paul Hindemith, during Germany's brief period of revolutionary ferment in the late twenties. Both Weill and Hindemith collaborated with him on a radio piece called *The Flight of the Lindberghs*, for example, about which he has this to say:

> *The Flight of the Lindberghs* is valueless unless learned from. It has no value as art which would justify any performance not intended for learning. It is an object of instruction…

Agit-prop such as this has a short-term propaganda value, but it finally defeats its own ends—by preaching only to the converted; and even to them it offers little more than a sanctimonious endorsement of received ideas. The rest of the audience is alienated and switches off.

Brecht soon came to desire an "alienation effect" in his work, but not at all in that sense; on the contrary, he meant by the term a form of theatre which invited the audience to switch on, mentally, to be alert and inquisitive. The alienation effect had to do with what he considered decadent about the post-Romantic boulevard theatre with which he had grown up—its narcotic torpor, the way in which its actors and audiences succumbed

[14]

together to a soporific state of near-trance, a hypnosis of the will, a wallow in the tepid waters of cheap emotionalism.

When he describes this, I always think of the cinema. And it does seem to me that Brechtianism has gradually prevailed worldwide, during the past half-century, in theatre design and direction and even architecture, at least partly because the cinema had already taken over that narcotic, dream-message function which it is far better equipped to perform, leaving the theatre free to flaunt its own machinery of artifice. At any rate, when we go to the theatre nowadays—those few of us who still do go—we accept that the spotlights may be in our full view, that the set will probably suggest a place and its significance, rather than merely attempting a convincing facsimile of reality, that the actors may appear in several disparate roles or perhaps comment on the action—that in these and a multitude of other ways, we will remain conscious of ourselves as an audience in a theatre at a certain remove from the presentation, scrutinising it analytically.

Which is not of course the full-blooded Epic Theatre of Brecht's vision but then that in itself was a volatile entity, constantly re-shaping and modifying itself in the course of his turbulent and itinerant career. For our purposes it is illuminating to observe the evolution of his attitude to a play as an "object of learning," in 1933, with Hitler's accession to power, he left Germany for a wandering exile which was to last until after the Second World War had ended. Around 1935, whilst living in Denmark, he had this to say in an essay entitled "Theatre For Pleasure Or Theatre For Instruction":

> Generally there is felt to be a very sharp distinction between learning and amusing oneself. The first may be useful, but only the second is pleasant. So we have to defend the Epic Theatre against the suspicion that it is a highly disagreeable, humourless, indeed strenuous affair. Well: all that can be said is that the contrast between learning and amusing oneself is not laid down by divine rule; it is not one that has always been and must continue to be.

He continues with the argument that (capitalist) society has rendered learning tedious by reducing knowledge, as peddled in educational institutions, to a mere commodity: but that it need not be so; because the social strata who are "waiting their turn," the discontented and dispossessed, are hungry for learning and will embrace it. In the same disingenuous vein, he concludes: "Thus the pleasure of learning depends on all sorts of things; but none the less there is such a thing as pleasurable learning, cheerful and militant learning." And then he adds, somewhat anxiously, "If there were not such amusement to be had from learning, the theatre's whole structure would unfit it for teaching."

This insistence that learning should and must and does contain its own amusement has a certain Roundhead ring to it. It is tautological to say that those who enjoy the processes of thought will find pleasure in ideas. But what of the others? Are they not to be allowed into the theatre? And even those who enjoy learning, might they not enjoy it more efficiently at a good evening class than amidst the paraphernalia of a stage presentation? What is the special extra thing which the theatre experience can offer them?

In a word, the thing is fun. And Brecht says so: frequently. It may surprise those who think of his theoretical writings as a mass of unrelieved turgidity to hear that the word *spass*—fun— resounds throughout them like a refrain. It occurs in an essay written at the very start of his career, prior to the production of his first play, *Baal*, when he describes the indifference felt by young writers like himself towards the established theatre practice of the day: "They can see at a glance that there is no possible way of getting any *fun* out of this." It occurs near the end of his career in 1953, when he is discussing why the Berliner Ensemble should produce *Coriolanus*: "We want to have and to communicate the fun of dealing with a slice of illuminated history." And it occurs at nearly every stage of his career in between, being accorded its maximum value in the

1948 synthesis of his mature ideas entitled *A Short Organum For The Theatre*, the fullest and most important of his treatises.

On the whole, this is not an aspect of Brechtianism which its adherents and heirs have chosen to emphasize. They have preferred as a legacy the Roundhead elements in the work of this complicated and contradictory genius. Such people do not just insist on plays as "objects of instruction," but their attitude to the audience is, I know what's good for you and by God I'm going to rub your snotty little noses in it. Certain of the committed playwrights who have been for some time a major post-Brechtian force in the contemporary English theatre express in their work an English version of this dogmatic, authoritarian, hectoring mentality, schoolmasterly in the bad old sense: certainly devoid of anything resembling fun; or in my view, education either.

The whole issue was reviewed by Brecht in a brilliant 1939 lecture, "On Experimental Theatre," which he delivered to a student audience in Stockholm. Significantly, it was given bang in the middle of that remarkable three-year period during which he wrote his trio of richly-textured, clear-sighted, subtle and large-scale masterpieces—*Galileo, Mother Courage* and *The Good Woman of Szechwan.*

The lecture begins by stating that the serious European drama has passed through two generations of experiment. Brecht summarises the experimentation as follows:

> In my view these experiments were pursued along two lines which occasionally intersected but can none the less be followed separately. They are defined by the two functions of *entertainment* and *instruction*; that is to say that the theatre organised experiments to increase its ability to amuse, and others which were intended to raise its value as education.

He goes on to review the two lines of experiment—which he perceives as never having properly fused together—dealing with his own contribution to them in a highly self-critical spirit. And he ends the lecture, not as a major figure of twentieth-century dramaturgy handing down the law to an audience of Swedish drama students, but as a bemused pioneer, still grappling with first principles, and formulating anew the central conundrum of his vocation with an eloquence which reverberates across the intervening near half-century:

> How can the theatre be both instructive and entertaining? How can it be divorced from spiritual dope traffic and turned from a home of illusions to a home of experiences? How can the unfree, ignorant man of our century, with his thirst for freedom and his hunger for knowledge; how can the tortured and heroic, abused and ingenious, changeable and world-changing man of this great and ghastly century obtain his own theatre which will help him to master the world and himself?

As a playwright who joined the game in the middle of the seventies, I have enjoyed access to an outlet which was denied to Brecht, and yet which is arguably a quintessentially Brechtian medium. Just as Strindberg and the authors of Victorian melodrama anticipated the techniques of the silent cinema, so a case can be made that Brecht anticipated television: if not in practice, then at least in theory. Marshall McLuhan's definition of television as a "cool" medium is surely another version of the alienation effect. We scrutinise the television screen as individuals, not as an undifferentiated mob. We adopt a stance which is casual, detached, sceptical, and yet capable of engagement, of emotional response, as well as of commentary and analysis. As for the playwright, not only is he able to address through television a mass audience of three or seven or twelve million people, he does so on precisely the same terms as a sporting event or variety show, and is in fact likely to be sandwiched between examples of each.

But is television merely another kind of spiritual dope traffic, a home of illusions—or can it be a home of experiences? Is it twentieth-century man's own theatre which will help him to master the world and himself?

These questions remain as rhetorical as when Brecht posed them about the theatre of the playhouse in 1939. The jury is still out. We know that television can be stupefying narcotic. We also know that television drama can effect some change, at least on a single issue, as (most famously) with Jeremy Sandford's 1960's play *Cathy Come Home*, which brought about the formation of the housing charity Shelter. We know that it can dangerously inflame an already violent situation, as in countless instances on the streets of this province. We also know that it can move whole nations and continents to contribute scores of millions of pounds to the alleviation of a human catastrophe, as has been achieved recently for the victims of African famine by the Live Aid and Sports Aid movement.

It seems that television partakes of the neutrality of Play itself. "Play" (so Huizinga tells us) "lies outside morals. In itself it is neither good nor bad."

Meanwhile the playwright's access to television is hedged about with constraints. He enters the technology as an invited guest and not by right. His work is filtered through a succession of intermediaries, script editor, producer, departmental head, and so on, before it even reaches the hands of its interpreters, the director, with his designer and cameraman and army of technicians, and then eventually the actors ... it must be made to fit precisely into a time slot. It must not offend too grossly the sensibilities of the average suburban living-room into which it will be beamed. And since the making of it will anyway consume a quite colossal sum of money, it must hold itself in readiness for radical changes dictated not by aesthetic but by cash considerations.

Apart from all that, I love working in television. And I don't understand how any serious playwright in this day and age can fail to rise to the challenge of it. It is not merely the great popular medium of the time, it is part of the fabric of people's lives to a degree which is unprecedented; it is not merely the real national theatre, but a multi-national one to boot.

[19]

How would Brecht have dealt with television? What would he have written for it? The obvious irony is that, whatever he would have written, it would almost certainly not have been seen on the screens of the German Democratic Republic where he elected to end his days—but might well have scooped up an armful of awards on Channel 4.

Even this would not have deterred him. His greatest gift was for survival. I suspect that he would have embraced the crass exuberance of commercials and game shows, partly to subvert their intentions but mainly for the mischief of it. In his *Short Organum*, he finally allots fun the pride of place in his grand scheme:

> From the first it has been the theatre's business to entertain people, as it also has of all the other arts. It is this business which always gives it its particular dignity; it needs no other passport than fun, but this it has got to have … Nothing needs less justification than pleasure.

Later on in the unfolding exposition, Brecht ties his love both of fun and of intellectual enquiry into the idea of play with which I prefaced this investigation:

> For although we cannot bother (theatre) with the raw material of knowledge in all its variety, which would stop it from being enjoyable, it is still free to find enjoyment in teaching and inquiring. It constructs its workable representations of society, which are then in a position to influence society, wholly and entirely as a game.

We have come a long way from a play as an "object of instruction" pure and simple: clearly, the way in which drama functions is neither pure nor simple. Brecht still believes in it as an instructive force for change, a means by which workable representations of society may be constructed—but entirely in a spirit at play. The didactic impulse is still present, but it has been wholly subsumed in the ludic one. Nowhere is this more fully achieved than in his 1944 play, *The Caucasian Chalk Circle*, which is imbued with a spirit of playfulness and indeed gamesmanship from beginning to end.

But of course the danger remains that the audience may simply take the fun and leave the message on the plate. It is almost certainly this process which allows, for example, the didactic farces of the Italian Marxist playwright Dario Fo to enjoy long runs in the capitalistic West End; and it is part and parcel of that whole conundrum which Brecht never entirely resolved, even to his own satisfaction.

Nevertheless, he has bequeathed to us a sense of drama as a potentially dynamic force in society, as a medium political by its very nature, as a forum in which ideas may thrive and be communicated. His influence is everywhere evident in the theatre of these last few decades of the century. As is the influence of that other major figure whose work also unleashed its power to astonish us during the nineteen fifties: Samuel Beckett, eighty years old and still with us—at least insofar as he has ever been with us.

What a contrast to Brecht he offers! Where Brecht's theoretical writings run to seven volumes, Beckett's consist of a single blank sheet. Where Brecht sustained the Aristotelian view of story as the heart of the drama—and conceived his finest plays as narratives of a spiritual journey, in the tradition of Everyman—Beckett abandons story altogether. In fact, his first and greatest play offers us the very antithesis of a spiritual journey: two tramps, suspended in limbo, endlessly waiting for somebody called Godot who never turns up. If Brecht was a Marxist missionary, Beckett is an agnostic monk. His work displays not the slightest inclination to teach or instruct anybody about anything. Far from constructing a workable representation of society, it shows us surreal and only semi-human figures, reduced perhaps to a trunk buried up to the waist or a dimly-lit hooded figure or an isolated mouth, sealed off in some undefined nightmarish space.

In all these ways and others, Beckett's work is at an opposite pole to Brecht's: and yet its effect upon us has been equally profound, and it has altered our perception of the nature of drama in at least equal measure. But how do we even manage to bracket them together in the same profession and perform their works in the same playhouses?

Well, Beckett is certainly at one with Brecht to this extent: he expresses himself through play. The title of his second piece for the stage makes this explicit:

> Old endgame lost of old, play and lose and have done with losing.

But Beckett's exercise of the play faculty is far more thoroughgoing than Brecht's: in effect, it determines the whole shape and tone of his work and also constitutes its subject matter.

To indicate what I mean—and also because connotations of frivolity and infantilism continue to cling to the word "play" in our work-ethic culture—let me quote again from Huizinga's book. Having disposed of the various utilitarian explanations for play in his opening pages, and having established fun as a quintessential element in it, he goes on to say:

> But in acknowledging play you acknowledge mind, for whatever else play is, it is not matter ... From the point of view of a world wholly determined by the operation of blind forces, play would be altogether superfluous. Play only becomes possible, thinkable and understandable when an influx of *mind* breaks down the absolute determinism of the cosmos. The very existence of play continually confirms the supralogical nature of the human situation ... We play and know that we play, so we must be more than merely rational beings, for play is irrational.

Consider Beckett's work in the light of these remarks. He presents us with stark images of a world which does appear to be determined by the operation of blind forces, beyond the control and comprehension of its inhabitants. Nevertheless they while away their time in it playing games, verbal and physical, games of repetition and reminiscence, little ritual games, often mordantly humorous. And this activity exercises the last remaining faculty which keeps them human. It is irrational, but their very awareness of this confirms that mind still functions in them. It is the one thing which holds the absolute determinism of the cosmos at bay. Once this capacity for play is lost, however much a burden or a torment it may be to them, humanity itself will be extinct.

How can we entertain in the theatre such a bleak view of the human situation, let alone be entertained by it? At some level the truth of Beckett's vision strikes home to us: we recognise it and acknowledge it, and are even amused by our recognition and acknowledgement. It illumines our inner life, the life of the spirit in the nuclear age, and it does so by means of play. It exercises the very faculty in us which it dramatises in its characters. It is thereby a civilising force: bleak but bracing. The term Theatre of the Absurd has adhered to it, but I should like to rename it Theatre of the Ludicrous—ludicrous being another word derived from the Latin *ludere*, to play.

We can hardly call Beckett's visions a form of instruction or teaching. But perhaps they can be characterised, in the broadest sense, as a form of education. They show us a truth and leave us to make of it what we will. But in the very showing, they furnish us with some tools of the imagination with which to grapple with our own predicament.

Beckett and Brecht, then, the twin colossi of the European theatre in this age, are not perhaps entirely poles apart. Nevertheless, they offer a formidable choice and challenge to those playwrights caught in their historical wake. The influence of each seems to me unavoidable, and yet neither offers a clear road ahead.

Let us now bring all this back home, to the demands of our own circumstances. What should drama be aiming to do in this society at this time? When I write a play for the BBC or for the theatre, should I be trying to instruct the public? If so, with what instructions should I issue them? Or should I rather be offering them an image of the interior landscape? Am I in any sense in the business of education?

I find myself thrown back on *Everyman* and the Christmas conjuring set by these questions. Since those days, I have been endeavouring somehow to discover or develop a form of drama for myself which can accommodate both these poles: the poetry and the trickery, the spiritual journey and the glitterball, the message and the sight-gag, the ludic and the ludicrous.

I am not a member of the party—any party—but there are political and social values which I wish to explore and promote in my work. Likewise, official versions of reality which strike me as malevolent or deceitful are constantly being promulgated by people in power; I want my work to offer alternative versions.

In a different vein, I am much obsessed by death; and by the spiritual void from which many of us have to confront it. Images present themselves to me in this regard which are beyond rationality, dragged on to the stage from the very borders of consciousness, powerfully charged for me in a way I cannot define.

In addition to all that, I am a strong adherent of fun.

All of this heterogeneous work constitutes self-education for me rather than any kind of tutorial for the audience: each of the plays is an entry in the private book of reckoning for my own journey. At the same time, my most fervent desire for them, once they're written, is that they give the audience a great night out, or in, as the case may be. They are in search of the truth and they aspire towards entertainment. All of this, however schizoid an impression it may convey, is by way of being a personal quest for inclusiveness, for synthesis.

A playwright should aim to be a truth-teller, a sceptic in a credulous world, but there has to be also an element of the medium in his make-up. He becomes possessed by other voices, both divine and diabolic, and they must be given their say: voices generated by the energy emanating from an intense moment of conflict, in a time and place, though the time and place is always here and now during performance. All plays are ghost plays. They issue forth and take their shape from a conflict within the writer himself, often a wrestling match between the soothsayer and the medium, mind and intuition. The most shapely plays emerge when the antagonists wrestle each other to a draw.

Plays should aim for the greatest possible clarity and simplicity, but not at the expense of their own intellectual integrity and truthfulness, which may turn out to be irreducibly convoluted and ambiguous. I am reminded of John Donne:

On a huge hill
Cragged, and steep, Truth stands, and he that will
Reach her, about must, and about must go.

There is a clarity which is false and a simplicity which is dangerous. The easy answer constitutes an artistic abdication.

Writing about and from within this particular place and time is an enterprise full of traps and snares. The raw material of drama is over-abundant here, easy pickings. Domestic bickering, street wit, tension in the shadows, patrolling soldiers, a fight, an explosion, a shot, a tragic death: another Ulster Play written. What statement has it made? That the situation is grim, that Catholics and Protestants hate each other, that it's all shocking and terribly sad, but that the human spirit is remarkably resilient for all that.

Such a play certainly reflects aspects of life here. But it fails to reflect adequately upon them. To borrow another dictum from Brecht, "If art reflects life, it does so with special mirrors." Documentary journalism can reflect with accuracy real lives being lived. Art amplifies and distorts, seeking to alter perceptions to a purpose. A play which reinforces complacent assumptions, which confirms lazy preconceptions, which fails to combine emotional honesty with coherent analysis, which goes in short for the easy answer, is in my view actually harmful.

And yet if ever a time and place cried out for the solace and rigour and passionate rejoinder of great drama, it is here and now. There is a whole culture to be achieved. The politicians, visionless almost to a man, are withdrawing into their sectarian stockades. It falls to the artists to construct a working model of wholeness by means of which this society can begin to hold up its head in the world.

A certain amount has been done. Alternative versions of the historical myths sacred to each of the communities have been staged: not in a spirit of mockery but in a spirit of realism, and out of a desire to substitute vibrant and authentic myths for the false and destructive ones on which we have been weaned.

Drama can do this and much more. It can contain the conflicts and contradictions, the cruelty and the killings, the implacable ghosts, the unending rancour, pettiness and meanness of spirit, the poverty of imagination and evasion of truth which unites our two communities in their compact of mutual impotence and sterility—all in a single image. Within that same single frame, it can demonstrate and celebrate a language as wholesome and nutritious as a wheaten farl, a stony wit and devious humour, an experiential vivacity and wholeheartedness, a true instinct for hospitality and generosity, which also and equally unite our two communities.

When we come to offer the audience an image of wholeness, we can cease the task of picking over the entrails of the past, and begin to hint at a vision of the future. Of course these are complementary parts of the one process. But I suspect that the useful time for history plays will draw to a close in due course. The challenge will be to find a belief in the future, and to express it with due defiance in the teeth of whatever gory chaos may meanwhile prevail.

The intentions of such work will be neither didactic nor absurdist. It will aim to inspire rather than to instruct, to offer ideas and attitudes in a spirit of critical enquiry, as a challenge rather than a riddle, and by means of this, above all, to assert the primacy of the play-impulse over the deathwish.

New forms are needed, forms of inclusiveness. The drama constantly demands that we re-invent it, that we transform it with new ways of showing, to cater adequately to the unique plight in which we find ourselves.

For those of us who find ourselves writing from within a life experience of this place, at this time, the demands could not be more formidable or more momentous.

Lecture given on 5th June 1986 at Queen's University Belfast.

PART TWO

Buntus Belfast

Last August was an infelicitous month for a Belfast prod who wanted to start learning Irish. Sam mentioned some ads in the Classifieds for classes in Divis Street. It would have been rather like taking a taxi into East Berlin for Beginner's Russian.

We opted instead for some place called the Rupert Stanley College of Further Education, a Corporation institute in Tower Street. It sounded very depressing, yet the very fact that Irish was listed as a subject seemed laudable and staked a claim on our support. Besides, it was in the industrial East End, where I was born and grew to immaturity, which I claimed to know like the back of my hand even whilst inwardly acknowledging that the backs of my hands were two pale and unobtrusive aliens to me. On enrolment night we drove down the Newtownards Road sporting a faint halo of earnestness and after-shave lotion. One end of Tower Street was barricaded: not to worry, barricades were ubiquitous, you grow to expect them. We drove in at the other end.

The Theatre of the Absurd has annexed the territory of farce and melodrama. It merely exhibits the violence in those genres from the anguished viewpoints of their protagonists. We had made our entrance into an Absurd drama.

On one side of the stage was the Rupert Stanley, an aluminium and glass facade behind iron railings. On the other stood a terrace of red-brick parlour houses. In the middle swarmed a small crowd which had turned into a herd of rhinoceroses. They were led by a great Bull Rhino who reeled up and down the street rending the air with his trumpetings. He was telling us to bugger off, to get our car the hell out of that or it'd be used as a barricade, but mostly he was just choking in agony on the jagged chunks of incoherent verbiage lodged in his throat.

A Little Man in a car downstage of us proffered the sop of his Shankill Road origins, but he might just as well have announced himself as Pope Paul. Meanwhile Sam slipped into the Rupert Stanley to enrol us in Irish for Beginners. He encountered a Nervous Official, called Berenger for all I know.

I sat in the tin shell of the car in the grip of a deeply irrational fear. I was a child again, with a dreadful secret swelling like a tumour inside me. Somehow the Bull would find out that I, born and raised a working-class loyalist, had come to the very heart of Ballymacarrett for the purpose of learning the Fenian's tongue. He would batter me into pulp. A Weird Sister loomed up. "Popeheads," she cackled, "they're all popeheads!" An Ingénue with pretty brown legs in a blue miniskirt was lifting an immense coil of barbed wire from the concrete front garden of a house. Her brother appeared with planks. They were going to close the street. Don't let any more of them cars in! screeched their Rhino Mother.

I realise now, though, that I was not in fear of the Bull at all, I was responding to his fear. For it was not hatred that had swept the herd but panic, the atavistic panic of the Northern prod, the panic, very like drowning, of a man heavily gravid with brawling emotions and thoughts which he has not the fluency to deliver, a panic that still crawls around in there underneath the weighty luggage of my education. The working-class prod is a verbal cripple and Doctor Paisley is his crippled dancer. No one else but the Doctor speaks for him and he cannot speak for himself.

For days on end I had listened to the pirate radios: from Free Belfast, eloquent political homilies full of agricultural wit and passion alternating with passionate witty folk-songs full of eloquence; from Orange Lil and Roaring Meg, tongue-snared bluster alternating with The Sash and God Save the Queen, repeated and repeated like an incurable stammer. If the

Northern prod is a villain, he is also often an unemployed labourer; likewise, the tide of history is flowing against him, but so is the slick suavity of the media.

He has no Bernadette to feed to the television dream-machine, no one with her abrasive command of his Queen's English. "But nobody understands us," my aunt had cried at me the week after I came home from America, and couldn't find the callousness or courage to point out that we don't understand ourselves, that we have no words to define the schisms that splinter every corner of our lives.

Sam came back looking very un-enrolled. We made a fast exit, threw some drink down, and relaxed into hysteria.

I had thought my motives for wanting to learn Irish were simple, but they're a coil of barbed wire in themselves. There was, of course, Mr. William's the milkman, who took my wife aside the day before we left America and said reverentially, "Mrs. Parker, will you do something for me ... will you say: 'God be with you till we meet again' in Irish?" But there was something even deeper and it had to do with origins. Could it be that I had ceased to turn my back now and, through literary sentimentality, had turned Republican instead?

That is what most Northern prod writers and intellectuals have done in the past. Their theory has been cultural homogeneity, but their reality has been a sense of inferiority to the "real" Ireland, a hatred of Belfast, a wistful reverence for the mountainy folk. However, my problem is that I feel an almost Oedipal obsession with Belfast. The city has stuck to me like a burr on my sleeve that no amount of flapping will dislodge. I cannot sink my identity in Dublin, nor in New York or Toronto, or London or Glasgow either, for it is skulking somewhere in the fierce, drab, absurd streets of Belfast which was once Beal Feirste, and that's why I'm learning Irish.

The taig gazes over his shoulder at the Dail while the prod turns his face towards Buckingham P., but they both know secretly that their corporate soul is out there somewhere in No Man's Land. Until it is located and defined, talk of the reunification of Ireland is, empty. Not until the North can put words to its sense of selfhood will the island become united again, whether the Border goes or stays. The effort will be harder for the prod, there are so many things for him to learn (like Irish), but it will be subtler for the taig, since what he has to find out is altogether less easily described.

We eventually found a class, in that final sanctuary of the middle-class refugee, the Queen's University Extramural Department, under the patient guidance of our excellent teacher Sean Phillips. We have come to accept the fact that you cannot, under any circumstances, aspirate and eclipse a word simultaneously. Sam and I are enthusiasts but half the others vanished over the Christmas break.

A classmate I was sorry to lose was a black student whom I kept meeting on buses. Each time we would have the same prodigiously inane conversation in halting Irish, astonishing the other passengers, who seemed to take it for Swahili.

When I think of that experience, I think of Myles na gCopaleen from Strabane. He was my final reason for learning Irish.

Irish Times, 28th January 1970.

Chickens on Parade in Belfast, USA

It's always startling to come across your name in an unexpected context, and the same thing applies to the name of your home town. Accordingly I did a double-take when I saw "Belfast" on a map of New England, perched half-way up the Maine coast. I pointed it out to my wife. We decided to visit it.

Driving through the outskirts, we could see from the big white colonial mansions that it had been a place of some importance in the nineteenth century. Its importance had clearly derived from its position at the head of Penobscot Bay.

But the sailing ships, except for Navy cadets and inquisitive tourists, were long vanished and the town had to seek income from a source other than shipping.

Here already was a parallel with our own Belfast. Except that in the case of Belfast, Maine, the new industry was broiler chickens.

American small towns have a fierce pride. They like to be peerless in some way. Belfast Maine announced itself to us as "The Broiler Chicken Capital of the World." Not only that, but we had arrived in town, by lucky accident, on the eve of the annual Broiler Chicken Festival, the town's great day—July 9.

As we picked a spot on Main Street under a shady tree to watch the parade, the coincidence of the date suddenly struck me. Three thousand miles over the nearby water, the Orangemen were only three days away from their Long March to Finaghy. The Boyne Water on one hand, Broiler Chickens on the other; there you have the difference between the Old World and the New in a nutshell.

The parade had a bit of everything. It was led by the local police chief and the fire engine, followed by the Governor of the State of Maine and Miss Broiler Chicken Festival, waving regally from an open car.

There followed a series of floats, the first of which was evidently a hardy annual, an immense effigy of a cheery hen with a bright red opening and shutting mouth.

Commerce figured prominently. The local chapter of the Shriners, one of those bizarre American male freemasonries— the Elks and the Oddfellows are two others—appeared riding in circles on a fleet of Hondas, each member wearing his fez.

The customary joke car drove crazily by, bucking up on its back wheels. And inter alia were the girl scouts, the High School band, the drum majorettes, the Army cadets; in short the whole panoply of rural America.

It was corny and colourful and just as ridiculous and enjoyable as our own public ceremonials.

The last item of all was a gigantic lorry full of cages containing actual chickens. When the parade reached Belfast City Park, these were destined to be slaughtered, barbecued and consumed by the festive populace. But we passed up this spectacle in favour of a visit to the local library to find out what we could about the origins of the town.

The elderly library ladies got into a flutter when we announced ourselves. They kept presenting us to passing townsfolk as "a couple from Belfast Ireland." In the intervals between, we managed to riffle through the dusty pages of the town history and extract the instructive tale of its inception.

The adjoining state of New Hampshire was largely settled before Maine because the latter was rugged and impenetrable. Many of the settlers were from Ulster. Later we were to drive through villages in New Hampshire called Antrim, Hillsboro … and Londonderry.

It was from this Londonderry, in 1770, that a small group of men made a pioneer trek to the Maine coast and decided to found a settlement there. All of them were Ulstermen, all but one from Derry, and all but one in favour of naming the new settlement Londonderry also. The odd man out was a Belfast man called James Miller. He wanted the name of the new town to be Belfast.

Most men would have bowed to the majority, but James Miller was stubborn. Like many of his fellow-countrymen past and future, he had no respect for compromise. He insisted that they toss for it. And that's how the future Broiler Chicken Capital of the World got its name.

On our way out of Belfast, we stopped at a roadside botanical and taxi dermal exhibit called Perry's Nuthouse.

Belfast News Letter, 21st February 1970.

An Ulster Volunteer

Nearly every day now in the North, the plea goes out to "forget the past." Such advice is both impracticable and pernicious. On the one hand, you can't forget a nightmare while you are still dreaming it. On the other, it is survival through comprehension that is healthy, not survival through amnesia. Besides, the past is not a dead letter. The past is explosive cargo in everybody's family dresser. Your grandfather is the past.

My own grandfather was three years old when Lord Randolph Churchill played the Orange card and the Unionist Party was born. He was ten when Gladstone introduced his Second Home Rule Bill. And he was twenty-nine when he signed the Ulster Covenant in the Belfast City Hall. Politically I should think of him as the honest Protestant working man, deluded and exploited by the Orange and Tory gentry and their military-industrial complex but it isn't easy to think politically of your grandfather.

He is a small man, spry and upright, but forced to shuffle a little by the enormous wounds in his thighs and calves. He chuckles a lot, says "ospital" and "threevin" for "dreaming"; he is shy, proud and alone. And all his life he has thought of Roman Catholics as a feared and deadly enemy. When I quiz him about the past, I feel like a hapless, insatiable detective, cross-examining the victim of a vast crime.

The leg wounds were decorations awarded in the vicinity of the Passchendaele Ridge and Hellfire Corner. They killed a football career which had started with a local team in Ormeau Park and gone on to playing for Glentoran—East Belfast's team—and for Ireland.

But there was no bitterness at this loss. Playing for the Glens and getting the Hun on the run were just two aspects of community: going to church, marching on the Twelfth, and joining the Ulster Volunteer Force were three others.

He has often told me with gusto about April 24, 1914, the night when the U.V.F. ran guns into Larne from Hamburg. He was summoned to Willowfield Hall, H.Q. of the East Belfast Volunteers, and then marched down to the Musgrave Channel. In the classic role of the universal soldier, he had no idea what it was all about till later. Carson and Craig and the other Lilliputian grandees were playing their chess game with Asquith's Liberals, and my grandfather's company performed night manoeuvres with their temporarily wooden rifles, closely observed by a contingent of policemen; one set of pawns an unwitting decoy for the other.

The past appears to us over our shoulder, caught in the distorting mirror of the present. The present has its own U.V.F., a kind of Harold Pinter invention, men with sticks of gelignite playing blind man's bluff, adrift in a world which has forgotten the way to get back home. The world's nerve began to shatter in this manner with the First World War, and it is impossible really to recover the lost era beyond that apocalypse in which the original U.V.F. flourished.

But I imagine my grandfather and his cronies to have been earnest young men, full of certainties and zeal, readers of books like *Thrift* and *Self-Help* by Samuel Smiles, not wishing to ape the gentry but respecting its superiority, wishing merely to elevate their family's station from a kitchen house to one with a parlour, scullery and pantry too, and an inside lavatory; which my grandfather did; and all his life he eschewed strong drink and tobacco.

The citizen armies of the South must have been filled with identical recruits. I imagine, too, that the old Volunteers had a Kiplingesque sense of romance and honour and valour. And that this was the emotional baggage that they carried into the carnage towards which their Imperial masters directed them.

As far as I can tell, my grandfather only hated the Germans in the way that St. George hated the dragon. Were his feelings towards Catholics of the same ilk? The subject is taboo.

Derry, Aughrim, the Boyne … and the Somme. This conjunction still thrives in Shankill Road folklore. How a battle fought against Germany in alliance with France became an item in the historical crusade against Papists is part of the cruel joke that fate and politics played on my grandfather and his like-minded contemporaries. The Empire clashed with a rival empire: Kitchener said to Craig "I want the Ulster Volunteers"; and that Good Fairy turned them with his magic wand into the 36th (Ulster) Division of the British New Armies. The East Belfast Volunteers metamorphosed into the 8th Battalion Royal Irish Rifles and marched off to Ballykinlar to train where my grandfather recalls being told by an officer that he wasn't really supposed to wear his U.V.F. cap anymore.

The Division went to the Western Front, straddled the River Ancre, and on July 1st, fought in its first battle. Official accounts report that the men were conscious of the significance of the date—the anniversary of the Boyne—that they shouted "No Surrender!" going over the top, that some even wore Orange sashes. Such stories may be true, though it's also true that their propagation serves a familiar purpose.

What is incontrovertible of course, is that the Battle of the Somme was one of the most appalling slaughterhouses in human history, that five and a half thousand Ulstermen were butchered in the thirty-six hours of their fighting, many of them Catholics and that all the ground they won was later re-taken.

My grandfather missed all that. Before the Division had left England for France he had been ordered back to the Sirocco works: the war machine demanded more munitions. But in 1917 he was recalled into the army.

He has forgotten the names of the battles. What he remembers is the rifle springing out of his hands when the shell exploded near him, the two corpses in the trench beside whom he was placed, the awful noise of the support artillery passing over his head, the officer who covered him "with a Jerry coat" because he was shivering. At the dressing station the surgeon left him till the end, taking him for a German on account of the coat.

He remembers the matron who walked down the ward one morning pointing at various men and saying, "You're for Blighty. You're for Blighty. And you're for Blighty." They were slid down a chute into the deafening hold of a cattle boat.

He remembers waking up howling out of a dream one night in the hospital at Cardiff, and the Scots amputee beside him saying: "My God. Pat, I thought they were on top of us again." And he remembers asking to be transferred to the U.V.F. Hospital in Belfast and being surprised that the doctor had never heard of it.

Wearing carpet slippers, with blood oozing through the dressings, he somehow made it to Liverpool and got the boat to Belfast, to his wife and seven children.

During the Troubles of 1920-22, 150 men were wounded by gun shot in East Belfast and 32 killed. My grandfather narrowly missed being the thirty-third. As he was walking to work along the Catholic Short Strand one day, a man appeared and shouted: "Run Jimmy!" Shots passed him as he ran. It's a commonplace story.

His life since then has been relatively uneventful. He had reached his forties, had proudly seen the inception of the State of Northern Ireland, and was content to raise his family, do his job and attend his Orange Lodge.

For a while after Paisley came to prominence, my grandfather spoke warmly in his favour. Nowadays he neither follows the news nor offers views on it. When I left his house the other day, he was standing in the gloaming of his kitchen. Beside him on the table was a pamphlet, posted by the Government to every household to explain the reform programme. It was called "The Way Ahead."

Irish Times, 6th March 1970.

School for Revolution

The trials of American radicals for political protests are constantly making news. What never makes news is the postscript to many of them. The warm television cables are coiled, the press phone in their story and have a drink … and the defendants are driven off to prison for one or three or seven years of limbo. Society abruptly transmutes them from showbiz celebrities into invisible men. Yet it is in the prisons and not in the courthouses that part of the destiny of the country is being spun.

The prison that I got to know is a showpiece of progressive penology, the Allenwood Prison Camp set in a magnificent blue valley in Pennsylvania. Expressing the impulse of society, it too is invisible. The Cornell University colleague who first drove me to it had been there before, but even so drove past the entrance twice. For there is no spiked wall, no dungeon grille, no guards or dogs—just a flimsy wire fence and a driveway shared with a golf club and a gate you open and close yourself. The acreage of woods and fields surrounding the handful of prison buildings is immense. My friend preferred to say that there is infinite room for expansion.

The prisoners—the preferred word is "inmates"—have a choice of working on the prison farm or in the factory. They live in communal dormitories and they have baseball and softball facilities and an Education Building. Education was our pretext for being there.

It is to Allenwood that most of the young convicted draft resisters in the East are sent, being good security risks. Virtually all of them are students or recent graduates. Each of them has burnt his draft card or sent it back to his Selective Service office, or maybe refused to take the acquiescent step forward in the induction ceremony into the army.

To provide them with an intellectual lifeline and to express solidarity, six Cornell teachers had arranged a rota of classes in the prison, each of us making the 3½ hour journey there every fortnight. My class, shared with another English teacher, was just called "Writing."

The first thing we discovered on arrival was that twelve of the most able political prisoners had been moved. They had gone on strike to protest against what they considered to be meaningless work and unduly harsh treatment. It was later confirmed by other prisoners that wardens would strike draft resisters because they knew they were pacifists. At any rate, the strikers had been whisked off to the State penitentiary at nearby Lewisburg.

It transpired that Allenwood was only a small branch of the penitentiary, a kind of suburb of the prison ghetto, a reward which could be granted or withdrawn. Lewisburg was the real prison, a cautionary Victorian fortress known to the inmates as "The Wall."

In the totalitarian society of a prison, truth is elusive. Nothing can be verified. We were forbidden to bring in anything except textbooks, and work written by inmates had to be scrutinised by the Education Officer before being taken away. This meant that a piece in which the inmate was candid about the prison never got beyond the classroom door. The writer either concealed it or destroyed it. One such piece dealt with a group of dormitories in Lewisburg known as "the jungle." The old lags who lived there were notoriously homosexual. The writer claimed that the threat of removal to "the jungle" was used against the dissenting young draft resisters; and he detailed cases of the threat being carried out, followed by the subsequent rape and hospitalisation of the victims.

The prisoner's only recourse is to write to his Congressman, who receives hundreds of letters from prisoners, mostly pleading wrongful conviction and is unlikely to do anything about any of them. There's also the press; articles could be smuggled out. But without solid verification no paper would be keen to publish them.

The *New York Times* has occasionally printed articles by released draft resisters, but most are afraid of making things tougher for their comrades still inside. Besides, the public demands no more for its prison taxes than invisibility: prison reform wins few votes, and young radicals are nationally reviled.

In all these respects, the prison presents itself to the political inmate as merely an intensified microcosm of society, a society which he sees governed by the "soft" dictatorship of big business, a warmongering society whose demands on his youth and courage he has defiantly refused. If he goes to prison a radical, he is likely to leave it a revolutionary. The process gains momentum from the ironic fact that prisons are perhaps the most fully integrated institutions in the country.

In planning the classes, it hadn't occurred to us that the "ordinary" prisoners might be attracted to them. In the event, they outnumbered the draft resisters, and black faces outnumbered white.

The Black prisoners were serving time for narcotics offences, confidence tricks and suchlike. All of them had a passionate political commitment and no matter how the classes started out, they nearly always resolved into a noisy, volatile debate about Black oppression. One scrofulous old conman, Ed Brockington, took the view that all Black politicians, policemen, bourgeoisie, businessmen and teachers should be shot as traitors to their people: how the revolution should proceed thereafter was cloudy. From the other end of the intellectual spectrum came passages out of Malcolm X and Franz Fanon.

A couple of the Black inmates were really talented writers, but they eschewed formal genres just as Eldridge Cleaver has done. Their writing was not a glory ticket or a substitute confessional, it was a function of survival.

Frank Smalls, a mean, towering man in his late thirties, had been in prison all over the country. In solitary confinement, he had flushed his writings down the lavatory. At night, in the dark, he had scrawled for hours, unable to see either pen or paper. The writing gave shape to the raw, restless monologue in his mind. He wrote about growing up scared amongst the "white eyes," about the attitudes of white girls he had known ("the paleface steppers"), about his disillusionment with Black Christianity "...which is nothin' but a dream of some guy flyin' out of the sky saying, 'Put on brakes, m.f., you have done enough to them.'"

The monologue was largely directed at white society, and in its threats and its pleas and its curious tone of intimacy was embodied the whole emotional complex of race relations in America: "Can you dig it-will you dig it-the flies and worms will eat you-can you dig-can you-you can-but you won't you damn fool."

When his work was read aloud in Allenwood, the white draft resisters sat silent. They were learning something that their fellow students at Cornell couldn't learn, for the latter had only people like me to teach them. The prison and the university had changed roles. And every time that American society unwittingly matriculates a student into this novel form of schooling, she contributes to her own disintegration.

Irish Times, 7th April 1970.

It's a Bad Scene, Mrs. Worthington

In the fifties, British theatre rediscovered realism. In the sixties American theatre rediscovered expressionism.

There's a connection with television. In its early days, like the novel and photography, it had seemed to be the supreme documentary medium, the apotheosis of realism. But in America, even early on, it was more like Pictures to Blow Your Mind By, and with the arrival of the Vietnam Show, the surreal blitz took over completely. You could switch rapidly through twelve channels, splicing a Right Guard commercial/a Kennedy dying/Cancer Society commercial/Lucky Strike commercial/a Pinkville/a Nixon commercial, and so on till you unhinged. If you stayed on one channel, it just took a bit longer.

The American theatre wanted to be "better" than television, just as it had yearned to be better than the cinema. It knew that television was the open wound through which the tormented American psyche drained all through the day and night. Very well, the theatre would be doubly surreal, but it wouldn't just bleed, *it* would also diagnose and prescribe. Mostly, though, it would bleed.

Available for sainthood were the mad French Artaud of the thirties, and the Contemporary Pole Grotowski, with his new religion of theatre and his impenetrable exegesis of it. Starting from Off Off Broadway, the movement spread to Off Broadway and eventually to the actual dread avenue itself. Across the nation, groups sprang up doing Street Theatre, Guerrilla Theatre, Total Theatre. Last November it finally reached Belfast as a Festival event.

At its best, this work reclaims crafts of the theatre that had been surrendered—dance, acrobatics, mime, choric chanting, striptease. Its best is the original La Mama troupe and the Open Theatre, both of New York. The former's production of Jean-Claude Van Itallie's *America Hurrah* deserves some of its acclaim. Van Itallie is a European who grew up in America: he is both casualty and onlooker, both dreaming the nightmare and tabulating it. He shows you the bestial horror of the motel room, but he stays in control of it with a steely, rational style. His is the orchestrated scream.

The Open Theatre's production of his *Serpent* was also worth it—but more for virtuosity in the crafts mentioned above (for example, a writhing hissing knot of actors which is both Tree of Knowledge and worm-clot) than for any important insight into original sin.

Van Itallie is a member of a group. He is a writer, and others in the group are actors, designers, choreographers, and so on. They collaborate: that is the Shakespearean way, the Chekhovian way, the way of ancient Greeks and medieval guilds, in fact the best possible way of developing a new and vital drama.

It is not, unfortunately, the way followed by the movement as a whole. Writers are shunned as wordbound, reactionary, stiff-limbed, and totalitarian: all of which they mostly are. So the actors overthrow their old dictator, and set up a groovy commune, because, actors are hip to where it's at, and with such pitifully limited equipment they create a similarly limited Statement about War and Sex. Bodies and nerves are unsheathed on stage and in the audience, to no particular avail. Far from being liberated, everybody gets more uptight, the whole exercise being more closely akin to current experiments in group therapy than to anything you might call art. These groups, like the hippies, are hag-ridden extensions of bourgeois America. Theirs is the castrated scream.

The Living Theatre is in the van, and has evolved a kind of "commedia dell'arte" which is lacking both in commedia and in arte: that being exactly the kind of crack that they despise. They have a point. Academic wit is often lipstick on a corpse. The trouble is, they exclude all forms of humour, in fact humour itself. During a performance of *Mysteries and Smaller Pieces*, one of them sits on the stage chanting things like Freedom Now, Fuck for Peace, Ban the Bomb, Abolish Money, for about twenty five minutes. I've remembered this because my companion retorted "Fuck for Money," thus providing the evening's only moment of truly living theatre.

Years ago, Clive Exton wrote a T.V. play, a fearless satire on television contest shows, starring Peter Sallis as a Hughie Greene figure. There was an eating contest scene, for example, where one of the gross contestants dies and is hurriedly whisked off camera. The Wherehouse La Mama's *Hilton Keen Show* was even worse than this. It was like showing fuzzy old lantern slides of Soho to the inhabitants of Sodom and Gomorrah. A satirist's talent is for walking into the enemy arena and winning hands down with his opponent's chosen weapons; then walking away whistling. This task will never be accomplished by a committee of actors. Especially against an enemy who is beyond defeat.

Little Mother by Ross Alexander was the only one of the group's three shows that came near to working, because it was the only one that was written. It was crudely and carelessly written, but at least you could sense a mind at work. *Groupjuice* was the identikit Total Theatre offering. Formally, it was mostly a series of inflated acting exercises, such as you can see any morning in the rehearsal room of a good repertory company. Thematically, like the bulk of science fiction, it turned out to be an endorsement of all the things that mother taught us: sex gets exploited, war is wrong, advertising peddles fantasies, you should develop your individuality, love is all you need.

I would rather do almost anything than go to the theatre these days. Most people concur with that, often secretly, I'm convinced. The new expressionism shuns the writer, the old realism dissatisfies him, and anyway the glossy theatre museums consider him an unthinkable economic risk. You go to the museum and see an ingeniously mounted Shakespeare or Strindberg or Shaw. You stand on the thick carpet in the interval gulping down a drink. People all around are talking about the actors and the set. You know that this is not your spiritual home. You know it isn't Shakespeare's or Strindberg's or Shaw's either.

The theatre is permanently in crisis. It is the most volatile and the least perfectible of all the arts. Why persist in returning to the whore? Because—whenever she's depressive she's as low as you can go, but whenever she's manic, she laughs all the other arts to scorn.

If that's ever to happen again, writers will need to reconstruct the theatre from scratch. Locked out by both the establishment and the anti-establishment, they will have to begin from their own bodies, their own voices and friends. They may well fall on their faces, like everybody from Addison to T. S. Eliot. All the same, in so doing, they may rediscover the sources of their poetry and their fictions.

Then at least we might have a worthwhile literature.

Honest Ulsterman, 23 (May/June 1970).

The Tribe and Thompson

I have a vivid memory of the first production of *Over the Bridge* in the Old Empire Theatre in 1960. My uncle took me to it. He was a shipwright and I was a Teenage Writer. It would be hard to say which of us was the more shattered by it. We were like members of a lost tribe, thrust before a mirror for the first time, scared and yet delighted by our images, sensing even then that they were much more than a mere reflection. And the mirror was no missionary trinket, but the work of a dues-paying member of the tribe, a man with the plain prod name of Sam Thompson.

There had been nothing in his background or circumstances to encourage him to write—no middleclass English teacher, no folk tradition or literary parents—nothing but instinct, which caused him to hoard up material for years, till at the age of 39 he was overheard talking in the Elbow Room by Sam Hanna Bell, the BBC Talks Producer, who told him to write it all down. The material stretched back to his earliest days in a kitchen house with four brothers and three sisters, their father a lamplighter. His fifth and sixth years had been lived in the midst of the sectarian murders and burnings of 1920-1922. At fourteen he had been apprenticed as a painter in the shipyard, and subsequently became involved in trade union work. In short, he was just like the man next door anywhere in East Belfast. Except that suddenly he had shattered us.

Five years later he was dead, and five momentous years after that the decade has closed and he begins to seem like its most important Irishman. For the tribe is now in the centre of the Irish arena. Its actions and feelings will crucially affect the future course of the country's history. Paisley is the cry of its blood and of the dark side of its mind, where race memories snout blindly around and psychic wounds cry like a child for succour. But Sam Thompson was the voice of the tribe's heart and its head, the voice of all that is civilised and decent in Belfast working-class life, the embodiment of its impassioned commonsense and derisive good nature. We would need his play if only to remind us that those life-affirming qualities exist and can triumph in the dreary claustrophobic warren of streets.

It may seem incongruous to write in this tremulous way of what Seamus Kelly's recent review called "an exposé of and a plea against the mindless murderous hatreds that poisoned his native city," but there you have the parody of art. A good production of a great play about hatred or despair can despatch you from the theatre walking on air. Despair is not inculcated by watching *Waiting for Godot*, but by watching, say, people on holiday: to be suicidally depressed about Ulster you must observe, not *Over The Bridge*, but Chichester-Clark sharing a joke with Paisley. Plays of this calibre do not "express" despair or hatred, they involve you in attitudes to those emotions. They conquer by defining them.

This is what invalidates two odd criticisms of the play that were mooted when Chloe Gibson's production was running in Belfast. One was that it had palled in comparison with the "real thing" that we now live with every day (walking out of the theatre I heard an explosion from the Woodstock Road). The other was that last August's celebrated mass meeting in the shipyard which declared for peace had rendered the play redundant.

Maybe such misconceptions are the effect of television saturation, stunting people's responses to the point where they confuse an artefact with a facsimile. The "real thing" (and the newsreels of it) is chaotic flux, overwhelmingly meaningless. Drama rescues us from the chaos by giving it a shape and a pattern, affording us insights and a saving chance to contemplate them. The shape that *Over The Bridge* has is virtually ritualistic, and its pattern approaches allegory. It consequently sends down emotional tendrils to such depths of the understanding of human nature as are undisturbed by topicalities. If the shipyard were to close down forever tomorrow morning—as it may well do, apparently—the play would continue to be as "relevant" as ever.

In Davy Mitchell, the old union leader, we have the force of good, unadulterated by human vices but enfeebled by the struggle with them in others. In the Mob Leader, whose cat-and-mouse scene with the embattled Catholic Worker Peter O'Boyle is the most gripping passage in the play, we have the unmitigated force of evil. These two emblems are in the middle-ground, establishing for us the twin poles of human behaviour. They do not contest directly with one another, but through the ruck of ordinary human beings, who are congenitally incapable both of sainthood and depravity, but keep seesawing between their own best instincts and worst failings. These are the characters who occupy the foreground, and they cover between them the whole Belfast spectrum. In Rabbie White, the "ruleatarian," there is the prototype for all spokesmen for citizen's defence committees, vigilante groups and tenants' associations: the crafty backstreet pedant, who is passionately in favour of a fair deal but refuses to see past the wee blue book of rules. In Archie Kerr and Peter O'Boyle are the representative prod and taig locked in their hoary squabble, the prod pigheaded and bullying, the taig shrill and querulous, neither prepared to bend a little … until the real violence starts, when each reveals too late his guarded reserve of moral courage.

All the characters fit into this pattern, but the most important of them to my mind is Warren Baxter, the young shop steward. He epitomises the process by which society here devours its young. His youthful emotion and energy is torn between the martyred idealism of his mentor Davy Mitchell and the status quo of sectarianism by which he determines to seek advancement as a realist and a "diplomat." All through the play he veers wildly between revulsion at the narrow-minded actions of the others and a sneering cynical acceptance of them. When the ritual act of violent death finally occurs, it is he who is forced to witness it, and witness also the silent majority walking away from it, not wanting to get involved. He describes this in the last speech of the play, a broken man reduced to total nihilistic impotence, who can give no answers. He has been scarred for life. There are thousands like him.

Few could quarrel now with that whole aspect of Sam Thompson's vision, though it was too much for the Unionist cultural establishment to cope with in 1957. But there is affirmation in the vision too, and my uncle and I responded to it at that first production without consciously knowing what it was. Speaking of his detractors, Sam once said: "They can't see that a writer like me may criticise his own people because he likes them very well." All through his work flows a swift deep current of love for his people and a conviction of their giant potential, thwarted though it has been down the years. They could produce a Davy Mitchell, of course, but a more typical product is Martha White, Rabbie's wife. Technically she has no business being in the play: the bulk of her part is taken up by a gabby awkward scene with Davy Mitchell's daughter at the end of Part One. But her role in the allegory is essential. Her voice expresses the neighbourly kindness, the rough-hewn wisdom and generous humour of the teeming street. There is nothing sentimental in this conception. She represents the human spirit's survival in the teeth of a lifetime of unemployment, T.B., overcrowding and religious derangement.

The same voice can be heard in "The Evangelist" in the character of Manser Brown, a part which was taken by Sam himself in the first production—fittingly, since it is the spirit which imbues all his work. He was his own best example.

A realisation of his full significance is beginning to dawn. Later this year, *Over The Bridge* will appear in book form, published by Gill and Macmillan, with photographs of Ballymacarrett, and a biographical introduction. R.T.E are to televise the play in September. I am hoping, with financial assistance from various sources, to edit all the rest of his work, produce a sizeable number of acting editions, and make them readily available to anybody interested.

All this activity can be traced back to one man, Brian Garrett, prominent member of the Society of Labour Lawyers and the N.I. Labour Party. He has been in charge of Sam's affairs since the playwright's death, and it is due to him that the name of Sam Thompson can now appear in the permanent repertoire of Irish drama, where it belongs.

Irish Times, 18th June 1970.

Introduction to Sam Thompson's *Over the Bridge*

During the Westminster election campaign of 1964, when Lord O'Neill of the Maine was still plain Captain at the Northern Irish helm, he made reference to "a certain Mr Sam Thompson whose past experience is, I gather, in producing works of fiction." A lot of blood has since flowed under the bridge; it is a sarcasm to which posterity has not been kind.

Bridges are a favourite Ulster metaphor. "Bridge-building between the communities" has become the compulsory sport of our captains and our kings. The traditional sport of stirring up sectarian hatreds, however, continues to be played at times of stress, like election campaigns, or when deciding upon a suitably provocative name for an actual steel and concrete bridge. Going Over the Bridge is another activity entirely, demanding a degree of guts, and an integrity which public life in Ireland has failed to cultivate, to say the least.

Sam Thompson dedicated his life to it. He coaxed, commanded, persuaded and implored his mulish fellow countrymen to make the journey. He wasn't a captain or a king but a shipyard painter and they listened to him. They knew the reality of his fictions.

The reality is there today on the wall opposite 2 Montrose Street in East Belfast: NO POPE HERE, TAIGS KEEP OUT, REM. 1690. He was born in number 2 in that other slogan-weary year of 1916, the seventh child of a lamplighter. Nothing distinguishes the street from thousands of other Victorian backstreets in Belfast; it has the same sense of torsion, the same decaying Lilliputian houses. When you enter it, the long narrow gully of red brick clenches you like a fist. The sky at the end of it is fuller than ever of shipyard gantries.

His responses to this environment were embodied in his radio feature *The Long Back Street*. It begins when he is six years old, sitting with his mother and sisters in the glimmering light of the gas mantle, waiting for his father to return from the round of his lamps. They play at guessing the identity of motor engines passing in the night—a military lorry, a police tender, "a lancy car rounding up the curfew strays." It is 1922, and over 180 people have been killed or wounded in East Belfast and the shipyard during two years of bloody turmoil between Protestants and Catholics triggered by the partitioning of Ireland. The Newtownards Road is pitted with the burnt-out shells of houses and spirit stores. The detritus of looting litters the back entries. The child has watched a man being kicked to death.

But "...although there was an atmosphere of violence all around us, it never entered our home. My parents hated violence..." In place of the scar of bitterness there was bequeathed a constructive anger. And this same principle applied to the impoverished hardship of life, for Mr Thompson was the part-time sexton of St Clement's Church of Ireland and the extra few shillings saved his family from the humiliations of the pawnshop, the tick men, the church handout of harvest loaves and the desperate refuge of the deadly "red biddy." Already at school the sensitive eye of the playwright was observing his mates who hadn't a penny for the gas and coal fund shivering miserably at the back of the room

He saw right from the start that poverty and sectarian violence were root and branch of the one ugly tree. Towards the end of *The Long Back Street* there is an election street-corner rally, in which the usual Unionist hack is whipping up the crowd with the familiar demented slogans featuring Popery and the glorious siege of Derry. From the back of the crowd comes a lone dissenting shout: "You can't ate Derry's walls when you're hungry."

Such a sentiment led him into the classes of the National Council of Labour Colleges after he had followed his four brothers into a shipyard trade at the age of fourteen. In 1939 he attended a N.C.L.C. summer school in Paris. But he had learned already what socialist theory he needed. The voice from the back of the crowd said it all.

After the war he became a painter for Belfast Corporation and a shop steward in his union. His wife May, whom he married in 1947, recalls another bridge anecdote from that time. The underside of the Albert Bridge needed constant re-painting, a dirty unpleasant job which entailed standing knee-deep in water. Among the squad of Corporation painters certain men somehow never got assigned to this particular job whilst others unfailingly did. Shop Steward Thompson negotiated a rota system involving one and all equally. Activities of this kind led to his being paid off, and he worked independently for a period in partnership with another painter.

It was not until he was thirty-nine years old that he started to transmute all this into writing. After his marriage he had moved across town to his wife's family house at Craigmore Street, which is near the BBC The local pub was frequented by radio and television people. One night he was overheard by Sam Hanna Bell, a BBC Talks Producer, telling shipyard stories. Bell told him to write it all down, and invited him to help out on a radio feature about the yard called *The Island Men*. In the next several years Sam Hanna Bell was to produce some half dozen Sam Thompson radio features.

Felicitous as this kind of catalyst is, it does not in itself account for a man's becoming a writer. All his life Sam Thompson had been half-consciously storing material, his imagination hibernating whilst his body and mind met the harsh demands of working-class life. He had often said, as so many people do, "some day I'll write all this down." But if making "works of fiction" is not treated as an honest day's work in western society at large, in Northern Ireland it's scarcely countenanced as a furtive hobby. His triumph was to demonstrate that the act of writing is possible even from deep down the mines of what he nicknamed "the Siberia of the arts." He was a bona fide prophet without so much as an honorary degree in divinity. He was far too much for the Belfast cultural establishment and it has never been the same since his eruption, thank God.

Over the Bridge was written between 1955 and 1957 and was his first work for the stage. He had done a little acting by this time in his radio features and in the theatre, and he grew friendly with many of the actors of the Group Theatre which was the only decent professional company in the province. Most of the Ulster actors of current international standing started their careers in the Group: the part of Rabbie White was conceived with J.G. Devlin in mind, and when the play was accepted for production by the theatre, direction was in the hands of James Ellis.

The directors of the theatre were rather less talented than their company. With rehearsals in full swing they requested the playwright to make changes in his script. The playwright naturally declined. The production was axed. Like Samson, Sam Thompson brought the theatre tumbling down along with him.

A public statement issued later by the board of directors defended its action as follows:

> [We] are determined not to mount any play which would offend or affront the religious or political beliefs or sensibilities of the man in the street of any denomination or class in the community and which would give rise to sectarian or political controversy of an extreme nature.

This staggering repudiation of drama as a serious art form explains why the Council for the Encouragement of Music and the Arts—whose chairman was also chairman at the Group and head of the local BBC—was renamed Council for the

Encouragement of the Migration of Artists by the indefatigable playwright. It was a repudiation that has become familiar in the history of Irish drama, and the definitive comment on it is Yeats's "On those that hated *The Playboy of the Western World* 1907":

Once, when midnight smote the air,
Eunuchs ran through Hell and met
On every crowded street to stare
Upon great Juan riding by;
Even like these to rail and sweat
Staring upon his sinewy thigh.

The railing and sweating went on for three frustrated years. Three directors and most of the Group company resigned, controversy raged in the press and in political circles and a breach of contract action was settled to the playwright's advantage out of court. Meanwhile his work lay unproduced. Finally he and the core of the renegade actors from the Group formed Ulster Bridge Productions Ltd., hired the Empire Theatre, and opened the play there on 26 January 1960. It was a momentous success. church

In Northern Ireland we have neither religion nor politics, but only a kind of fog of religi-otics which seeps in everywhere. To be a writer is to be a public figure, up there in the trenches with the captains and the clergymen. Sam Thompson fully accepted this and he roamed about fearlessly in no-man's-land waving a red flag: it was and is almost impossible to think of his work in aesthetic terms, to divorce it from its social and historical context. In 1960 that context was mostly obscure outside Ireland, and when the play moved to London's West End after breaking box-office records in Belfast and Dublin, it was withdrawn after a couple of performances. The English reviewer who most nearly touched its significance was J. W. Lambert in *The Sunday Times*: "Homely, humorous and free from the faintest whiff of propaganda, Mr Thompson's play shines with simple virtues and is very welcome." Nobody could know, least of all a dyspeptic West End audience, that the play was in on the birth of a new era in Irish history, inaugurating a decade which was to explode its content across their television screens.

But the insight of Mr Lambert's comment is that unlike most Belfast examples of the printed word, the play is not a tract. Its virtues are movingly simple, but they are far from simple-minded. They are essentially the virtues of the medieval morality play, *Everyman*: commonsense, a fundamental decency, implacable honesty, a natural dignity which is rooted in a clear-eyed and impassioned vision of moral behaviour. The premise of the play has the same brand of simplicity, saying in effect: there were sectarian pogroms in the shipyard in 1920-1922 and in 1935; all their elements are thriving still; here's how it could happen again.

Propaganda trades in abstractions, but *Over the Bridge* deals in people. It shows them doing something universal in a particular context—failing to cope with the ideals of their own institutions. Christian love and trade union brotherliness founder on the rock of each character's selfishness or greed or other squalid inadequacy. The thoroughly good man, Davy Mitchell (based on a real union leader of the thirties, David Scarborough) is as ineffectual as *Everyman*'s Good Deeds, who is

so weak
that she can neither go nor speak.

At the opposite pole the Mob Leader, quintessence of the evil in human nature, has a chilling strength. In between are ranged the others, with their various ways of failing.

The English they all speak is the plain lean language of the Belfast streets, with its earnestness, harshness, and keenly funny sense of irony, very far removed from the soaring dialect extravaganzas of O'Casey and Synge and yet as distinctively Irish for all that, and a vibrant flexible instrument in the mouths of actors. It was a dialogue that came readily to hand for the author.

In June 1961 he suffered his first heart attack, exactly two years after taking up writing full time. In November he suffered his second. He didn't take kindly to sickness. As soon as he was on his feet again, he would resume the full round of acting on stage and television, lecturing, campaigning and finishing his second play, *The Evangelist*, which received production in Dublin and Belfast the same year, again to popular acclaim. In 1962 he collapsed again.

His third play, *Cemented with Love*, was written for television, and it dealt with gerrymandering, personation, smear tactics, or as the author put it, "everything that goes on here at election time." It was drafted before the 1964 election Campaign in which he ran as a Labour candidate in Down, an extraordinarily unsuitable rural seat which he had no chance of winning despite a colourful and hard-fought campaign. *Cemented with Love*, which had been scheduled by the BBC for transmission in September, was unaccountably postponed after work had started on its production. A certain aura of *déja vu* prevailed. In December it was postponed again. There was now no doubt in anybody's mind that political pressures were at work, despite the BBC's protestations to the contrary.

On 15 February 1965, Sam Thompson died in the offices of the Northern Ireland Labour Party. The play was finally televised two months later. His death was a grievous loss to Irish drama, for there is no doubt that he had many plays still in him. His last and as yet unproduced work, *The Masquerade*, was an attempt at a new departure, with a London setting and an experimental form. The three that reached the stage in his lifetime contain his complete diagnosis of Ulster's disease. *Over the Bridge* shows sectarianism worming its way through people's working lives, *The Evangelist* uncovers the fanaticism and hypocrisy deforming their religion, and *Cemented with Love* the appalling corruption of their traditional political parties, Unionist and Nationalist.

He has never been needed more than in the dark days since his death. The painful missing factor in the whole Ulster equation is a sane and compassionate leader for the Protestant working class. There is no knowing how Sam Thompson would have fared in this perhaps impossible position, but he remains the nearest thing to such a man that we have yet seen.

There can be no doubt that his work contributed to that extraordinary mass meeting in the shipyard of 15 August 1969, at which the 8,000 workers, brought together by their shop stewards in the midst of renewed civil anarchy and bloodshed, voted in favour of maintaining "peace and goodwill in the yard and throughout the province."

His spirit survives and it survives most powerfully in his plays and particularly in *Over the Bridge*. Like any true writer, it was in his work that he really lived, and still lives.

Sam Thompson, *Over the Bridge* (Dublin: Gill and Macmillan, 1970).

The Green Light

FX Blitz (Fade under)

PARKER: East Belfast was bombed in the Spring of 1941, and I wasn't born until October of that year. I don't know how I come to carry an image in my head of crowding into the air-raid shelter with all our neighbours. Maybe it's true that memories begin in the womb. More likely I dreamed the scene so intensely, it became true: and this kind of truth, the truth of memory and of literature, is more important than the trivial reality of what actually happened.

The air-raid shelter sat out in the middle of the street, its gloom heavy with furtive bodies and the smell of urine. Let it be a symbol of the past. I was drawn to it. But my nightmares had me entering it, to be terrorstruck by a man with a knife coming at me from a dank corner. The day they demolished it I was both glad and disturbed.

FX Bomb

PARKER: A great metal ball thundered into its concrete hide, exposing the mangled iron bones.

I don't remember rationing, but I remember the bomb crater. That was the uncomprehending name by which we knew the pond we played in. It was in fact a water-filled crater, caused by a bomb intended for Shorts aircraft factory. We got frogspawn there, and one day we launched a raft and fished out the red cylinder of the bomb itself, and threw it around till we got bored.

FX Children playing

PARKER: The war was just spent relics and we were the children of the new age.

Once the whole of East Belfast had been a pond. The Lough's waves lapped up against the steep ridge which is now crowned by the Holywood Road, and the ridge is in fact a raised beach. I learned all this years later in grammar school. When the sea retreated, it left the flat mud and plain that was to become the industrial warren of Ballymacarrett and its extension Sydenham, where I lived. Man himself continued the process by reclaiming land. When lorries went up our street loaded with excavated earth for reclamation, I made a friend of one of the drivers, and talked him into letting me go with him to the dumping site. I had to crouch down in the cabin in case the inspector at the gate saw me, with my head jammed beside the thudding gear lever.

FX Tip up lorry dumping earth—engine noise

PARKER: At the water's edge I watched the earth slowly tip as the lorry's back rose up whining on its greasy sliver pole.

The whole trip was a form of mystery and romance—not the kind that library books are classified under—but the spiritual kind that every human being craves as much as he craves lunch.

Years later I was to find the supreme expression of this unnameable hunger in Scott Fitzgerald's novel *The Great Gatsby*. I was tantalised by a sense of wonder, an intimation of perfection, as Gatsby is by the green light across the bay from his estate.

We lived in Sydenham till I was seven. At the bottom of the street, the trains to and from Bangor rattled past. Beyond the tracks rose the inevitable gantries of Queen's Island.

Three sounds were constantly in the air. There was the industrial noise, first of all: the distant clanging of the shipyard and the sudden roar from the test bench at Shorts.

FX Shipyard clanging and aircraft roar

PARKER: Then there were the baleful moans of foghorns from ships coming up the lough.

FX Foghorns

PARKER: These sounds were vaguely exciting; they etched in the universe of which our street was the centre. But the folksy sound that will now most effectively reclaim that submerged landscape of childhood for me is a street cry.

FX Street cry — hawkers etc.

PARKER: There seemed to be dozens of hawkers then, all with ponies and carts. Women would come out in their slippers with the hearth brush to sweep up the horse's droppings for garden manure. There was the rag and bone man, the herring man, the balloon man with his hordes of plastic windmills and those paper rolls that squawk and snake out when you blow into them. I can whip up a feeble and foolish nostalgia for all this now. Not so for the coalbrick man, though, flying past covered in black dust, surrounded by the steam curling from the coalbrick he sat on, like a devil rising from the pit.

FX Coalbrick man calling

PARKER: Somehow he had become identified in my mind with Kibby. Kibby was the bogey man into whose vile power our mothers threatened to deliver us when they had reached the end, as they put it, of their tether.

I hope I never feel again the quality of terror that Kibby inspired in me. The emotions of my childhood were all brute primary colours. They were so stark that joy was almost insupportable as despair. It was mainly for this reason that I longed to grow up and was glad and relieved when I finally did.

But the foghorns and the street hawkers and my father's choir group called the Sundowners who practised regularly at our house—these were the ingredients of romance that nourished my imagination. There were other things too, like the bell of our church.

FX Bell of St. Brendan the Navigator church

PARKER: It was an old ship's bell because we belonged to the parish of St. Brendan the Navigator. I liked the pictures of him, sitting in his curragh—which I thought then was circular—in the middle of waves and leviathans. He was my one slight contact as a child with the invisible Celtic world of Ballymacarrett and Connsbrook and Connsbridge and the rest of Ireland beyond: an unsuspected skeleton under all the familiar surfaces. And the bell had glamour even though it tormented me many's a Sunday as I ran down Connsbrook Avenue with a stitch in my side, trying to get to Morning Service before it stopped ringing. I liked it because it had been the tongue of a ship once and had the sound of voyage in it.

So far as what went on inside the church was concerned, I'm afraid I had the same reaction to it as to school: I shrank away in revulsion.

FX Anglican liturgy

PARKER: The Anglican liturgy is vigorous and sonorous poetry, but all it meant to me then was clothing my legs in the icy sandpaper of pinstripe trousers, and sitting in the cheerless gloom surrounded by people mumbling a form of words neither meant nor understood.

However church was nothing compared to life in school. This school was permeated with a heavy odour of depravity and madness, actually embodied in the foetid stench that hung in the air of the dining hall.

The headmaster was a Dickensian nightmare of fondling obesity and prurience. The janitor was finally dismissed for assaulting a little girl. The teachers were likely to be faith healers or alcoholics; one elderly lady whose white powdered face I won't forget was a casebook sadist who sliced a ruler across your cold knuckles at every opportunity.

Added to this there was of course the usual jungle law of youngsters in a tough neighbourhood. I was in poor shape for this, being not only a weakling but a coward as well. A coward as far as aggression goes anyway; somehow I could always find courage to suffer, but never to fight. I managed to stay out of trouble by being harmless and unobtrusive most of the time, but it's almost obligatory, isn't it, to tell the story of the time you stood up to the school bully. So here it is.

He was on the steps outside the main door of the school. As I wheeled my bike through the door he jeered at me. I hit him in the chest with all the force of a powder puff. He shoved me, casually, and I fell over backwards, sprawling down the steps tangled up in my bike. I got up and cycled home, my throat choked with spiky stalks.

In spite of all that, I might have learned something at school—for I had one nice motherly teacher—if it hadn't been that the teaching itself was an entirely behaviourist system of rewards and punishments. This teacher had little certificates called Honour Cards which she awarded for various achievements such as clean teeth and nails, combed hair free of nits, politeness, tidy jotter, Arithmetic, English, and so on. The anxiety of competition for these cards was intense, the agony of disappointment—or of elation—devastating. This system for producing adult emotional cripples appears to be even more extreme today than it was then. Later, in more congenial surroundings, I learnt to play the system, even to the point of winning that ultimate Honour Card, a university degree, for having a combed mind and tidy memory. Now I'm busy trying to unlearn that very skill, to gear my mind to some healthier system.

There were things that I enjoyed at school, of course. Notably there were the school broadcasts.

FX School broadcast: music and movement

PARKER: The Music and Movement series afforded us the physical release of tumbling, whirling and falling about the room. I remember too an enthralling series in which a commentator pretended to be set down on the planet in various moments of prehistory, and described all that he could see. For a brief spell in these broadcasts I could dismount the treadmill of achievement and indulge my imagination. But the rest of the time it had to be held inside like a swelling, dangerous secret.

When I was seven I got sunstroke at Helen's Bay. It's probably been my most remarkable achievement to date. The skin on my back shed itself in curling white fronds. Pleurisy set in, and I was off school for a year, mooning over old comics up in the back room.

Illnesses are presumably accidents and yet it amazes me how they seem to have woven themselves symmetrically into the design of my growing up. Maybe I would have been a celebrated trick cyclist or an Olympic harrier if I hadn't had such a sickly constitution, but I doubt it. All my inclinations, from the cradle, were towards passivity, stoicism and reflectiveness, and they were merely intensified by years of not being allowed to work up a sweat or lie in the sun, of constant x-rays and waiting rooms pent up with blighted unhappy children. They were intensified too by Belfast itself, which often seems like one vast clinic, all dark windy corridors and huddled queues, and no doctors.

Partly because of my smitten lungs, the family decided to flit. We climbed the raised beach and forsook Sydenham for the more rarefied air across the Holywood Road. Suddenly we were semi-detached and suburban, and a piece was no longer a piece but a packed lunch. But we were also adjacent to green fields, to a sports club and the estates of the landed gentry.

These estates aroused in me, not an instinct for social equality, which was already strong, but a scientific curiosity. They were full of trees, shrubs, grasses and above all, birds. Along with a new friend, I became a raving ornithologist, binoculars, notebook and all. The identification of each new species occasioned a flurry of excitement and scribbling; we were dazzled by goldfinches, kingfishers, yellowhammers, and stopped dead by the sparrowhawk that suddenly swooped up along a hedgerow over our terrified faces. The old lady in the big house brought us in and showed us the greenfinches feeding at her windowsill. I had grandiose plans for a survey of all the trees in the old lady's estate, which would then be listed, sketched and described in a book I would present to her: characteristically, I never finished it. We did manage to persuade the Ulster Museum, though, that we had seen the rare Red-Necked Pharalope at Whitehouse, and we swelled like peacocks when it got a mention in one of their publications.

All the same, the supreme experience of our bird-watching mania was the first time we crawled out of bed in the dark in order to listen to the dawn chorus. We had built a tree platform at the edge of one of the estates. At three in the morning, we huddled there munching liquorice comfits, rain dripping heavily throughout the still forest. We shushed each other when a faint sound came filtering out of the far corner. It was a song thrush. And a wan streak of grey in the sky began to thin out the inky darkness. The singing caught us in its thrall, swelling and swelling with the growing light, till the whole forest was flooded with bright clamour.

FX Dawn chorus of birdsong

PARKER: At the time, though, the profound effect of the experience was strictly incidental. We were there as sibling scientists, recording information, like ornithologists all over the country, for the World Bird Observatory. That evening, we applied our synchronised watches to the gentler and more plangent phenomenon of the dusk chorus.

The following year, we elected to do an all-day survey of birdsong in a seaside habitat, and I cajoled my father into getting up at two in the morning and driving us to Kinnegar. When dawn came, we discovered that we'd pitched our tent on a rubbish dump. When we sipped our tea, we found that the water we'd made it with was salt. But we faithfully recorded every single chirp, trill, screech, pipe and wail we heard that day.

It may seem incongruous that the natural world and the countryside should present itself to a child as interesting machinery, while he should discover romance and mystery in the industrial city. But it has largely remained that way for me, a neat inversion of the Wordsworthian ethic.

At eleven I joined the Boy Scouts and started camping, and later I went youth hostelling, and this was all a great pleasure, but the pleasure lay in gaining control over practical matters, in changing from a "handless eejit" of a child into somebody who could fry an egg and fell a tree. Any emotional involvement with the environment, whether it was Loch Lomand or Whitepark Bay or the Northumberland fells, was secondary and just conventional. Later it became self-conscious and posturing for a while, when I was being filled up with Byron, Shelley and Keats at grammar school. I would stand on an utmost rock, striking a noble pose as immortal longings welled up in harmony with the thundering deep, fighting down the thought that my good suedes were getting ruined.

An example of what was really romantic was my older brother's records, scratchy 78's of people like Humphrey Littleton and Edmundo Ros and Les Paul and Mary Ford.

FX "Vaya con dios" sung by Les Paul & Mary Ford

PARKER: Meanwhile, I continued fraternising with interesting adults. The lorry driver in Sydenham was replaced by the workmen building the new estate we lived in. With remarkable forbearance, they allowed me to join them during their tea break, and even filled the tiny mug I brought. My distraught mother would roam in search of me, only to find me sitting with a gang of workmen outside a half-finished house, swilling tea. They were like urban gipsies to me.

Public events merely skirted the edge of this extremely self-absorbed world. The King died and the Queen was crowned, but more important to me in those weeks was the departure of my appendix. This event etched the world of hospitals on my mind, and I suppose I have believed ever since that hospitals hold the secret of the human condition. In the clinics of earlier years I was constantly falling desperately in love with little girls whose legs were in callipers or whose faces were badged with a livid rash. Now surrounded by them in hospital I was wracked with the same overpowering emotion, the heart's response to the absolute isolation of suffering, first your own and then other people's.

FX Coronation of Queen Elizabeth II

PARKER: I got out in time for the Coronation, shuffling feebly around bent double, an old man of eleven. There was red white and blue bunting in the garden, and I had diligently kept a Coronation scrapbook full of pudding-faced portraits of the regal couple and the happy family. It was rather like the Twelfth, only without the bonfires and without "the Men."

Which brings me to all those fashionable Ulster incidents: the time I got beat up by a Catholic gang, the love affair with a sweet Papist girl brutally crushed by intolerant parents, and so on. I haven't mentioned these yet because they never happened to me.

[71]

Fenians lived out beyond the stockade somewhere and went to chapels instead of churches and walked out of the pictures before the Queen was played. They were too abstract to interest me much. The Free State was where my mother got me slabs of pink bubble gum and sticks of rock with Dundalk or Omeath down the middle of them.

FX "Twelfth" — flute bands

PARKER: The Twelfth was fairly exciting, what with collecting wood for the bonfire and waving at my Uncle and Grandfather in the procession. All in all, my self-centredness was almost impregnable. At the same time, the accompanying introspection made me aware of the poison in the Ulster system and saved me from growing up to be that palsied surgeon, the liberal Unionist.

From wild birds I moved on to budgerigars, and it was in an aviary that my childhood came to an end. This aviary was a handsome construction of wood and wire netting, with a tree in the middle and a house with a sliding door for the birds to sleep in. It was built for me in the back garden by my father and contained eight or nine birds. They were a riot of colour and noise; walking home, I could hear them from a couple of streets away.

FX Nine budgerigars chirping

PARKER: For a while I lavished attention and affection on them but then I began to feel that dread secret ebbing of interest which I wouldn't even confess to myself. I got increasingly careless about cleaning out the aviary and filling their seed bowl. One morning the aviary was quiet. The birds were a gaudy heap of corpses.

It's improbable that they died from hunger and more likely that they were panicked into a suicidal frenzy by a cat on the roof. So my family tried to assure me. But the cause was irrelevant: I had neglected them and they were dead. I filled up with remorse until my joints actually ached. It was the last time I wept, the tears slowly tearing themselves one by one through the seared eyeballs. Speechlessly I got some twigs and cord to make crosses, dug a grave and buried the bundle of little albatrosses. The remorse went grinding on for days.

The whole experience was a form of birth trauma, an awakening to the terrible burden of being a free agent. At the same time the corresponding joys of this predicament were becoming apparent to me. I began a headlong gallop through about every human activity that gets described in books as a hobby. I built up a vast stamp collection and gave it away, I gardened just long enough to plant trees in the most awkward places, I plunged into a frenzy of woodwork and emerged with a rhomboid bookcase. I did chemistry experiments in the kitchen, learnt magic tricks and practical jokes, embroidered traycloths for a time, and having driven my parents to distraction, I then went to a Baptist tent mission and got saved and started conducting revivalist meetings in friends' garages.

I can reclaim only a fraction of those delirious fancies that carried me through puberty. There was a friend with whom I drew up plans for an ascent in a balloon, the balloon to be inflated with gas from our stove. And there was rock 'n roll.

FX Skiffle group

PARKER: I started a skiffle group called The Troubadours which performed at one or two church hall dances. Inevitably, my long-suffering father got implicated. I pestered him for a guitar until he finally built one for me. It was a vehicle of long hours of adolescent world-weariness up in my cold bedroom.

But all of that was really just preliminary scuffling. In the midst of it there was one activity stealthily creeping up on me, a driving force that would brook no rival as ingenuous as a hobby. It was the single mouth for all my hungers. It was not content to be a vocation, it insisted on being a job too, and finally a way of life. It was writing.

So imperceptibly did writing take possession of me, I have no idea of when it actually happened. By the age of fourteen I was turning out poems, by fifteen I was convinced it was my life's work, and by sixteen it had developed into a raging fever. This was, of course, paralleling the emotional graph of adolescence, which rose steeply under the pressure of life at school.

The primary school, as an appropriate final gesture, had failed to enter me for the 11-plus, and so I was shuttled into a secondary intermediate school. This was a great stroke of luck, for the two years that I spent there were the most productive of my whole education. The school was brand new, the teachers young and full of fresh idealism, and the English teacher and vice-principal is still one of my friends.

Suddenly all my quirky eccentricities were being encouraged: I was performing magic tricks for the class, organising a bird club and before very long acting the lead in the first school play. I can't imagine a better way of becoming intoxicated with the theatre than this was: playing Everyman at thirteen—and in a costume made by my father.

Everyman was probably the first work of literature to flood my mind with light. I'd never read any children's books, and very little fiction of any kind; instead, I'd read books I found around the house, like an account of a transatlantic crossing in a small boat and the autobiography of a man who'd lost both arms in the war. This medieval play was something new, the simplest of fables transmuted into high drama, the commonest of words transmuted into poetry. This miracle of transmutation was a part of the mystery I'd been in search of, the only philosopher's stone worth discovering. I've since encountered plenty of false metals, but they never fooled me for long because right from the start I knew the true gold: as in Death's words to Everyman:

Reader: over

What, thinkest thou thy life is given thee?
And thy worldly goods also?

I had thought so, verily.

Nay, nay, it was but lent thee!
For as soon as thou dost go,
Another awhile shall have it and then go therefro
Even as thou hast done.
Everyman, thou art mad. Thou hast thy wits five,
And here on earth will not amend thy life,
For suddenly do I come.

PARKER: Unfortunately, it became obvious from all this that I was, as they say, grammar school material. I was entered for the review exam and passed on to a small respectable grammar school outside Belfast. My status reversed from star to clod. I had two and a half years of Latin, French, History, Snobbery and Conformity to catch up on, just when I was on the verge of striking poses on the utmost rock and wrenching white hot poems from my steaming heart. The suicidal stuffiness and intellectual drudgery combined to make me resentful, morose, wretched and inwardly priggish and arrogant: in short, adolescent, but with a vengeance.

There was a crisis of faith to contend with too, of course, the terrible struggle between conscience and received belief. My conscience forbade me to speak in church any part of the Creed I couldn't accept any longer, and as the Sundays went by it became more and more pitted with gaps, phrases I would mouth but not speak. Finally there was nothing left but the first phrase, "I believe in God," and when that went, I quit. Before this, however, there was the anguish of Confirmation followed by first Communion. When I touched the symbol of Christ's blood to my lips, I fully expected some cataclysmic retribution on my hypocritical body. Things like that are so important when you're sixteen. It's a time of life I'm glad to have left behind.

The writing, the guitar outbursts, acting in the annual school Shakespeare production and going dancing—

FX Dance band—(Everly Brothers playing "Dream")

PARKER: these all helped to sustain a precarious emotional balance. The quest for romance had by now taken on a narrower meaning in the Saturday night dance ritual. Suddenly girls had flared through the five senses of my mates and me. Their scent, their dresses, their hair brushing us when we danced, it all dazed and disturbed us. All we talked about was the dance, and the talent or wenches or tarts, last week's and next week's. We twittered towards the dance like a flock lured on by instinct, and we stumbled back home, girlless and overstrung. We sensed a holy grail somewhere in the heat and press of bodies, in the pass-outs and ladies' choices and jive competitions. It goaded us on to dance after dance, we fretted for it the whole dreary week in school; every Saturday we set out to find it, at last, walking sometimes for three or four miles, our collars turned up jauntily, our conversation bawdy and boastful, but our hearts filled with trepidation and longing.

Every Easter we roared up to Portrush and charged around in ways that we thought outrageously licentious, useful raw material for the pulpit and the press. But it was all a form of playacting. Genuine sensuality would have shocked and terrified us. We were trapped in the cold wind that visitors to Portrush like to call "bracing," and it would take a great deal more than a dozen vodkas and a defloration in the sand dunes to release us from that.

My adolescence ended, almost too neatly, after I had made the great escape to university. It was as if all the frustrations, the spiritual oppression and drudgery had culminated in a physical canker. A bone tumour developed in my left leg, and the leg was amputated. I was maimed. But the process of coping with that reality developed or uncovered a stability and a serenity that I had desperately wanted for as long as I could remember. This only began to crystallise after a long period of confusion and darkness, but it became embodied for me early on in an otherwise insignificant piece of music. It was a track from a record I was given as a present in hospital, a record of Jimmy Raney, the American jazz guitarist. It didn't express resignation, and certainly not acceptance—but a wry, lyrical quietude. It was this that attracted me to it, and not the title of the song: "Everything Happens to Me"—

FX "Jimmy Raney in Paris" Vol.2

PARKER: What was left from the gone years was the desire to penetrate the heart of all mystery. I hadn't been able to name the vision that had drifted before me all through childhood and adolescence. I still have it and I still can't name it. But I feel its nature most poignantly in the closing sentences of *The Great Gatsby*, Fitzgerald's great novel. These words are my only excuse for making this excursion into personal history:

Reader:

He believed in the green light, the orgiastic future that year by year recedes before us. It eluded us then, but that's no matter—tomorrow we will run faster, stretch out our arms farther ... And one fine morning—
So we beat on, boats against the current, borne back ceaselessly into the past.

FX Prow of boat against lake or sea current.

An edited version of this script was broadcast with the title "Self Portrait" on 3rd October 1971 on Northern Ireland Home Service (Radio 4).

Exiles by James Joyce

The real test of a Joyce fanatic is not his acquaintance with *Finnegans Wake* but his familiarity with *Chamber Music* and *Exiles*. Many have taken a perfunctory glance at those gossamer lyrics and that dry, wordy Ibsenist play: few are intimately acquainted with either.

Exiles, in fact, has attracted less attention than anything else Joyce wrote. In its day (1916) it failed to achieve a major production. Yeats brought to bear on it the full intensity of his magisterial myopia and rejected it for the Abbey, as he was to do with equally interesting plays by Shaw and O'Casey.

Suddenly it has become a fashionable hit of the seventies, handsomely reprinted with an introduction by Padraic Colum and Joyce's own notes at the end. Why? Like Robin Maugham's *The Servant* and Nicholas Mosley's *Accident* and L.P. Hartley's *The Go-Between*, it has received the Harold Pinter Good Writing Seal of Approval—not this time by his making a screenplay out of it, but by his directing a West End production of it.

This all gives rise to a multitude of thoughts, of which the following are a few at random:

The theatre is an even chancier business than literature, for a published play is nothing more than a box of tricks stuck on a shelf waiting for somebody to haul it down and find a key to unlock it. Joyce has had to wait fifty-five years: what chance have the rest of us got?

Pinter was obviously attracted to the play by the compressed, almost gnomic dialogue, with its strange stylisation. It's symptomatic of the last and most extreme phase of Joyce's Dedalus vision of life before that was enveloped by the efflorescence of the Blooms.

Like all the best modern writers—Chekhov, Brecht, Eliot, Beckett—Joyce experimented in several forms. Furthermore, he was able to achieve the integrity of each form with a single work: *Portrait Of The Artist* is the consummate novel, *Dubliners* is the definitive short story collection, the contents of *Chamber Music* (whatever you think of their merit) are indisputably verse, and *Exiles* is wholly theatrical. Having taken the measure of these traditional (or at any rate nineteenth-century) categories, Joyce was able to move on to the massive and momentous synthesis of them which is *Ulysses*.

To get down to the actual play: if written today it would be called "Richard and Bertha and Robert and Beatrice." Richard Rowan is the Joyce-Dedalus protagonist who has spurned his country, his church and his dying mother to forge the uncreated conscience of his race. Nora Barnacle has been transmuted in to Bertha, the elegant, uneducated country girl who is living with him out of wedlock. With their little son Archie, they have returned to Dublin from exile in Italy.

In Joyce's story "The Dead," Gabriel and Gretta Conroy are essentially this same couple as they would have been had they married and stayed on in Dublin with the husband in a safe and respectable job. At the end of the story, Gabriel's sexual ardour is baffled and frustrated by his wife's sudden passionate outburst for a past lover who died from her repulse and lies buried under the nettles at Rahoon.

In *Exiles*, Bertha too mourns for a past lover. Robert Hand, a journalist and a friend from the old days, assumes wrongly that he is the man, and makes advances to her. She reports this to Richard who, whilst not exactly complaisant, tells her she must act only by her own free choice. Meanwhile, Beatrice Justice, a cousin of Hand's (the names are clearly emblematic) is in love with Richard with whom she has been carrying on an intellectual correspondence for some years.

The jealousy generated between the four of them propels the action along - but this account makes the play sound like a mere sexual intrigue, which it is far from being as Shakespeare's *Othello* (to which reference is made by Joyce in his notes). The central issue is indicated in the title: Richard and Bertha have returned from geographical exile, but Richard's search for a free life has led both them and their two supplicant devotees into a social and spiritual exile which threatens to estrange them even from each other.

The play has a very spare and static structure, like a late Ibsen play stripped of its buttressing symbolism. How much of its obscurity is due to a diffusion of unassimilated ideas could only be resolved by seeing a production. It would be interesting to know if *Exiles* has as yet received a professional Irish premiere.

Fortnight, 26th January 1972.

The Dream and After

"The dream is over/What can I say?" sang John Lennon in 1970, with a characteristic sense of timing (this was on his first, best solo effort, the "Plastic Ono Band" album). What he did in fact go on to say was that he no longer believed in a whole catalogue of things, from Buddha to the Beatles, from Kennedy to Elvis ... "I just believe in me." Thus, did the previous decade of rock music end with an act of renunciation from one of its brightest and best, and the present one begin with a characteristic retreat back into the self. Goodbye yellow brick road.

I started reviewing that same year, which is rather like becoming the life and soul of a party just as it begins to break up. Virtually everybody at the time had had an interest in the music—even if only in the Beatles—and for all my friends, the latest Who or Janis Joplin or Traffic or James Taylor album or concert was an event of major importance. There was a rough consensus of taste within a whole generation spanning Britain, Ireland and America as the producing countries—Belfast having contributed Van Morrison and Cork Rory Gallagher and Dublin a whole melee of young musicians in groups like Skid Row—and a large portion of the rest of the known world was in there rocking along.

And then the guests began to leave the party. Some went clutching their old Dylan and Joan Baez albums, others their old Cream and Hendrix. Still others crept away with nothing but their treasured and very old Eddie Cochrane and Buddy Holly discs. Many went empty-handed, to look for a job, organise an election, grow their own breakfasts, start a family

… too old to rock 'n' roll, too young to die. The number of people who wanted to hear about Stephen Stills's latest band, or get into reggae or listen to a terrific new English group like City Boy or borrow last week's *Rolling Stone* diminished steadily until it was down to the hard core of committed fans. Rock music, once the self-appointed purveyor to the Western world of mass cultural revolution, had shrunk into a minority pastime, on a par with macramé or trainspotting.

Some people called this growing up, but actually it was a breaking up into schismatic sects. And breaking up is hard to do, even though, like every mass movement, the rock culture had always contained hidden inner dissensions. It had all started in defiance: I'm old enough to remember a choleric headmaster storming into our classroom, ripping our Elvis poster off the wall and scrumpling it into the waste paper basket. That kind of behaviour engendered solidarity. Later I was able to win a school debate on modern culture single-handed by the simple expedience of illustrating my brief few words with a burst of Jerry Lee Lewis's "Whole Lotta Shakin' Goin' On." But even at university in the early sixties, it was still not entirely hip to be a rock 'n' roll fan. Blues, yes. Rhythm 'n' blues, even. But the Everly Brothers, I mean, let's face it … Could a fully grown adult sing "Be-bop a lu-la, she's my baby" without ridicule? Could an average white band really play the black and blues? Could Little Richard really play the piano? If you loved Fats Domino could you like Pat Boone? We suffered these and many similar dread doubts, but all in silence. In the face of condescension and even mockery, the ranks held firm.

Then suddenly Beatlemania and Dylanology struck, and over-night everybody agreed with us. It was all vindicated, the music was legit. There was a huge scramble for the bandwagon, rock 'n' rollers were given Orders of the British Empire and honorary doctorates from distinguished universities, professors wrote books, music critics gave talks on BBC Radio Three, concerts mushroomed into monster rallies, the theatre surrendered to rock, Jesus Christ himself became just another superstar, one of a hectic multitude.

For the body of the one true music was growing to immense proportions, and nobody could any longer embrace all of it. The doubts multiplied and the schisms began. There were those who just got sick of the whole circus and wanted to start from scratch again, to re-live their adolescence, jiving to Chuck Berry and Bo Diddley at the hop. These very same, now middle-aged gentlemen were trundled out to help launch a revival movement which was taken up by earnest young musicians who could have been Bill Haley's grandchildren, dedicating themselves to reproducing copies of the originals. Primitive rock 'n' roll thereby followed New Orleans jazz through the portals of the museum of living music.

Meanwhile, other veteran fans, wanting the music to grow rather than regress, gradually developed into a progressive splinter group; which itself naturally splintered further, some favouring protracted improvising, others electronics, still others jazz-rock. And the new teeny-boppers growing up were going for (what was to us) an increasingly more dreadful set of manufactured non-entities, from Boland through the Osmonds to the Rollers. Young mums and dads fell in with John Denver and Peter Sarstedt and the Carpenters, decadent sensation seekers followed Bowie and Alice Cooper and the New York Dolls and now Kiss. Then there were the country-pop people, the Kris Kristoffersons and Tanya Tuckers and Emmylou Harrises and the bib soul and disco market, and the new wave of bib-ballad romantics like Barry Manilow and Eric Carmen ... a proliferation of specialists. To love them all your taste would have to be not so much catholic as schizoid.

So the dream was indeed over, and it won't recur; not for our lot, certainly. The dream was a bit confused, like most dreams, but it definitely had to do with communality, everybody grooving to the same riff, everybody generating peace and love and joyous energy through the same music. It was a nice dream and not an altogether silly one. In fact it was very beneficial and I for one wouldn't have missed out on it for anything.

However … nostalgia definitely isn't what it used to be when people start looking back wistfully at the sixties. For the further those years recede, the more cheap and shallow and narcissistic and downright embarrassing they appear. Really, they were mainly remarkable for the final triumph of the admass, the victory of style over substance, of trend over conviction, of appearances over values. The seventies have been drab by contrast, defensive, uncertain, wracked by traumas. But on balance I prefer them in every way—including musically.

For a start, some of the people who got themselves established a decade ago have only really come into their own since 1970. It has been a thrilling experience to follow the careers of Paul Simon and Joni Mitchell, for instance, as they've refined the art of subjective songwriting to the point of astonishing subtlety and depth reached in their respective latest albums. It needed the years of reflective craftsmanship to produce such songs. Then also, a number of maverick new groups have emerged on both sides of the Atlantic, with the ability to straddle the great divide between the charts and the progressive sophisticates—bands like 10cc and Queen and Little Feat and the magnificent Steely Dan. These bands have sustained the very best qualities of sixties hard rock with a welcome added edge of self-deprecation and humour.

Even the reactionary developments have brought bonuses. Revivalism was fun enough until it played itself into stultifying boredom and self-indulgence; but it served to remind people that pop music hadn't started in 1962, or even 1955. The sixties had been so self-absorbed that they'd turned their back on the heritage. Now it was possible to place rock in the whole continuum of modern popular music, from Stephen Foster onwards, to discover ragtime and rediscover Gershwin and Rodgers and Hart and Tin Pan Alley and even Glenn Miller, though it all began to get faddy and whimsical again at that point.

But the richness of the whole multifarious tradition has become accessible to us in the last few years, and when added to the vast heterogeneous contemporary output, it means that nobody should ever be stuck for something to listen to. The music is there, alive and well, offering as much energy and solace and food for the soul as ever, keeping its devotees sane in a world unhinged. Today I bought the Sinatra/Rita Hayworth album of the musical "Pal Joey," watched "A Hard Day's Night" again on television and played albums by the Grateful Dead and the Beach Boys and John Lennon while writing this. A day like that can't be entirely in vain.

The richness of musical resources has fuelled the work of the McGarrigle sisters and Maria Muldaur, just to end with specific cases. For me, these are three of the most exciting artists currently popular. Kate and Anna McGarrigle have confirmed the impact of their brilliant debut album with their recent concerts in Dublin and London. Ms. Muldaur has dispelled any remaining doubts with her third album "Sweet Harmony." Their eclecticism, their maturity, their womanhood, their restraint, none of these qualities would have been valued ten years ago as they are today. Performers like these will never be superstars, of course, never play at some future Woodstock. But so long as that's okay with them, it's okay with me. I mean, it's only rock 'n' roll.

Irish Times, 18th August 1976.

Belfast Women: A Superior Brand of Dynamite

Personally, I love Belfast and hate it with an equal passion. In other words, it's my hometown. Growing up there in the '40s and '50s was like growing up in outer Greenland. I remember a school debate on the motion that the Irish Sea was wider than the Atlantic Ocean. Carried unanimously.

We were supposed to be British, but when you visited "the mainland" (an insult in itself) they took you for a Canadian or a Scot. We were also supposed to be Irish, but when you went over the border to Dundalk or Dublin, they treated you humorously, as an exotic alien.

We didn't have any country, we just had a Province. A very, very provincial Province—politically corrupt, culturally bankrupt, full of aggressive inferiority, sectarian, self-obsessed, and unutterably dreary.

I fled from it to America, in the time-honoured manner, as soon as I had finished university.

What a contrast! Cook-outs on the patio, skin-flicks in the drive-in. I saw the La Mama Company and the Newport Jazz Festival and student revolt and Little Richard and the Hollywood Bowl and Bobby Kennedy. An immense, noisy, rich cosmopolitan culture, bursting at the seams with vitality and madness. Instant gratification.

And in the middle of it all, I found myself inexplicably ruminating about Belfast. There was the other side to the old hometown, the rootedness, the sense of community, the way every conversation gets handled like a one-act play. And the pubs. Right from birth I'd been carrying on a private internal war with the place, and I needed to come to terms.

So in August 1969, I went home. Since I'd been away, some new ideas had crept in—like civil rights in politics, ecumenism in religion, takeovers and "rationalisation" in industry, permissiveness in morality. It was all too much, the Province was in no condition to take the strains. After a long slow simmer, the place exploded—the very week I came back. Barricades in the streets, gutted buildings, the Army everywhere and then gunfire at night.

This was no private war, this was bombs going off within yards of where you were sitting or walking, friends and neighbours shot at and killed, living on your nerves, a daily diet of horror.

It's in its eighth year now, and people have come to live with it, as they do with virtually anything. But living through it is not comparable with other people's war experiences on these islands. As Frank Stock (the main character in *Spokesong*) says to his grandfather, who is a Great War veteran: "It's not just the same as it was for you. There's no common enemy. There's no Back Home. No Boche. And no Blighty."

It's a family war, a house divided against itself. Any parked car, any shopping basket might kill you. The "enemy" might be the man you sit beside on the bus, or he might be lodged in your own breast, for many of the people are hopelessly torn between the points of view, helplessly schizoid in their attitudes to violence, the Border, the British, the whole frightening muddle.

Experience has made them that way; but you'd never know it from what you see on television. Which is normally some neanderthal "public representative" mouthing the same old blind stubborn dogmas. In the country of the confused, the one-track mind is king.

But then this desperate confusion and bewilderment felt by most ordinary Ulster people is only one truth among many which the media have failed to communicate to the outside

[87]

world. In fact, eight years' continual bombardment of the British public with information about Northern Ireland seems to have communicated very little of substance.

People I talk to in London are still extraordinarily hazy and confused and fed up about it all. They confuse Belfast with Dublin. They confuse the IRA and the UDA. Which suggests to me that "News" in itself is largely meaningless and that an overgrowth of this commodity finally defeats its own purpose; it muddles, frustrates and in the end anaesthetises the understanding.

Understanding is crucial. Certainly, sooner or later—I fear lately—all of us in Northern Ireland will have to wake up to our common identity (a new identity for most) and create some kind of political structure to accommodate it. But seven centuries of bloody history can't and won't be resolved overnight. It needs all the understanding, all the fortitude, all the imagination that the combined people of these islands can bring to bear on it.

Meanwhile, Belfast soldiers on. Some of the changes have been surprising. For example, from a position of extreme apathy the city has now probably a higher density of community associations than any other urban centre in the British Isles. The troubles have made people aware of how their lives are run, and governing institutions no longer have such an easy time imposing their will on communities. This year, a grandiose scheme for an elevated motorway ringing the city centre was defeated. I'm proud to say I participated in this victory, and you can hear a bit about it in the play, folks.

Some things don't change. There's still a ferocious inward-looking indifference to what goes on in other places. And even though you can't walk down a street any longer without bumping into a poet, the citizenry remains on the whole unimpressed by artistic achievement. The first three acquaintances I met on returning from the opening week in London made no allusion to *Spokesong*.

The only way your head's likely to get swelled in Belfast is if a building falls on it. We're down now to one theatre and five cinemas—that's counting the suburbs—and few people are really fussed about it. The remaining pubs remain packed and television consumption is at American levels. There has also been a resurgence of home entertainment: everything from people getting blotted on their own home brew, from traditional music sessions in the back kitchen or theatricals in the front parlour, to the quiet transformation of many innocuous terraced houses into massage parlours.

One thing the city can still glory in, and that's its women. A superior brand of dynamite. Argue about it all you like, but frankly they're more attractive than anywhere else I've ever been. It must have to do with the toughness of being a woman—and in a particularly unliberated society—allied to all the other rigours of growing up in the place. You need character to survive all that. And by God they've got it. Only a Belfast woman could have conceived the idea of a guerrilla peace campaign.

In fact, there are more admirable people in Belfast than you might have been led to believe, and I have the good fortune to number several of them as personal friends. It was for them and all those like them that I wrote *Spokesong*.

Evening Standard, 2nd November 1976.

State of Play

I have been making my living from writing for nearly ten years now, nine of which have been lived in Belfast. For the last couple of years I've been able to devote myself exclusively to writing plays. What follows is probably best described as reflections-in-progress.

To start with what I perceive as the strengths and weaknesses of theatre in Ireland: the strengths are in acting and writing, and the weaknesses in directing and criticism. Professional newspaper criticism is virtually non-existent. The average theatre reviewer in Dublin is generally a journalist whose actual area of expertise is agriculture, medicine or hurling. If your work fails to engage his interest, which is almost invariably the case, he will abuse you in print, in terms others might consider harsh for a child-molester or arsonist. As to directing, this is as often as not done by actors who have attained seniority or by guests flown in from abroad. There are very few full-time, skilled, artistic directors in Ireland.

In my view these weaknesses vitiate the strengths; such is the organic and collaborative nature of the theatre enterprise. When a critic of the stature of (say) Kenneth Tynan emerges, the whole theatrical climate in which he operates is affected, as it is when a director of the stature of Peter Brook emerges, to take another English example from the post-war period. Without collaboration and challenge of this quality, actors can grow coarse and lazy, and playwrights repetitive and ingrown. Which summarises pretty well the perennial condition of the Irish theatre, I think. The theatre culture is certainly rich, but it is not nutritious, because there are vital ingredients missing from it.

There is of course the case of Tyrone Guthrie, an Irish director of precisely the magnitude whose lack I've been bemoaning. But it is noteworthy that his theatrical legacy is to be found in England and Ontario and Minnesota rather than in Dublin or Belfast. I hope to return to this point at the end.

In the meantime, here's my major proposition: the absence of both a directorial and a critical tradition in the Irish theatre arises from its lack of any intellectual or theoretical foundations.

Consider the situation in some other countries. English theatre is of course grounded in Shakespeare and in the 300-year old canon of Shakespearean criticism and production. In contemporary plays like Stoppard's *Rosencrantz and Guildenstern Are Dead* and Edward Bond's *Bingo* and *Lear*, that tradition is affirmed by being challenged. Meanwhile the present generation of German playwrights is grappling with both the theoretical and practical legacy of Brecht. A Norwegian playwright could scarcely ignore Ibsenism. At the Moscow Arts Theatre, Stanislavski's productions of Chekhov can still be inspected. All of these are traditions grounded in theatrical revolutions, where a total view of the art was forged, encompassing its role in society as well as the shape of its stages and the style of its presentation, and so on.

I don't believe that such a total view was bequeathed to us by the national theatre movement of Yeats and Lady Gregory. To begin with the main impetus of their enterprise was a literary one, and its purely theatrical elements were drawn largely from the amateur drama movement. Nothing radically new in the way of *mise-en-scène* or acting style or mode of presentation was achieved, or at any rate nothing that has survived. The revolution was one of content but not of form. The total revolution which Yeats desired was not achieved, by his own admission. The Abbey was established as a writer's and actor's theatre of naturalistic comedy, and not as a director's or philosopher-showman's theatre, and so the pattern was set.

Yeats's writings on the theatre are the only substantial body of theory we have, unless you count Shaw's criticism, which in this case I don't, since it addresses itself almost entirely to the English theatre; although I must also own up to a personal distaste for the Shavian sensibility. Whilst admiring his crusade for a theatre of ideas, I find in his actual work merely a theatre of opinions. His characters to me are inhabited by right and wrong but not by good and evil.

Yeats's essays are excellent on the practical business of writing a play. Far from being a poet who failed to understand the theatre, Yeats was a poet who understood the theatre thoroughly, realized that as a popular medium it could not be made to accomplish his ends, and accordingly turned his back on it. The theories which he subsequently developed involving the use of masks, stylization of voice and gesture, the use of music and so on, are absorbing to study. But they constitute, in the context of this particular discussion, an impressive irrelevance.

Maybe I can illustrate the point. It is written into the constitution of the Lyric Players' Theatre in Belfast that every seasons's programme will include a Yeats production. This clause has been honoured every year for twenty-seven consecutive years now. Yet it's fair to say that in all that time the work on the Yeats plays has neither modified, related to, or informed in any way whatsoever the work during the rest of each season. The annual Yeats evening is an act of dutiful homage, and not the cornerstone of a whole theatre philosophy.

It could scarcely be otherwise. The national theatre movement found its mainstream in the great realist tragi-comedies of Synge and O'Casey. These plays and their later rowdy offspring from the pen of Brendan Behan are what most people mean when they use the words "Irish Drama."

Synge, in the brief prefaces which are the only commentary he vouchsafed to us, touched on the qualities for which these plays have become renowned: ripe and glorious colloquial language, an unsentimental and yet compassionate account of the lives of ordinary people—and characters, living those lives, speaking that language, who achieve a comedic greatness. The Irish public of course, true to form, didn't initially take to any of this. But they came round in time acknowledging the fact that they did at last have a national drama, and that it was a splendid one.

Synge died tragically early. O'Casey tried to move on. Without getting into the rights and wrongs of *The Silver Tassie* controversy—and it being an Irish fight, they tend to be very jumbled—I want to speculate on its implications. What strikes me is that O'Casey was clearly moving towards two kinds of playwriting which have been conspicuous by their absence in Ireland—experimentalism, and politically committed work (in the socialist sense). I go along with the majority view that his later plays are over-written and under-realised in comparison with his early realistic masterpieces. Whether they would have been better plays if the Abbey had accepted *The Silver Tassie* is very open to doubt. But at least experimental and committed playwriting would have entered the mainstream repertoire. And that would have prevented people like me from assailing yet again the profound suspicion of ideas in Irish culture, its conservatism, its self-satisfied provincialism.

The Abbey was not, of course, the only theatre in Ireland. There was most notably the Gate, and Denis Johnston, a playwright with a healthy disrespect for the Abbey pieties and an acquaintance with the wider reaches of European drama. But Denis Johnston was and is a maverick, and that is a word which seems to apply to almost all the interesting Irish dramatists from that day to this. There is very little in the way of continuity or underpinning. There is no body of received opinion. There is no continuing debate on the idea of a theatre. There is not even enough against which to rebel. There are no directors or critics. There are only maverick playwrights and good actors with bad habits.

But needless to say—and here I begin to show my hand—this situation is not without its advantages. Even if the national theatre movement had developed a coherent and successful theatre ideology, its politico-cultural motivation would have continued to dominate. It was a movement born of nationalist idealism and bred in a time of nationalist violence and political upheaval. In the North of Ireland, we have been living through another such time for the past decade. The nationalist ideal has not come out of it very well (nor of course has the unionist ideal—but it had hardly been notable in the past for sustaining the artistic impulse). A sense of passionate nationhood has not been evident in Irish writing for quite some time now. Romantic Ireland's dead and gone. Yet again.

Even before all that, and when I was most fully steeped in the words and works of Yeats and Synge and the rest, the nationalist rationale of the movement kept me at a distance. If you grow up an East Belfast Protestant, you scarcely acquire a clear sense of nationality, let alone nationalism. Both your Irishness and your Britishness are hedged about with ambivalence. (This may be why I feel such an affinity with the urban Jewish sensibility).

At any rate, the chief legacy of the Abbey tradition is spent begging the pardon of my friends and colleagues in the present Abbey company. And the defunct nature of this tradition permits me to beguile idle moments in lounge bars with a little romantic moonshine of my own. I can irritate Republican friends by claiming that my own work belongs in a venerable Anglo-Irish tradition of comedy of manners, stretching from Congreve and Farquhar through Sheridan and Goldsmith to Wilde and beyond—and that the national theatre movement was merely a temporary aberration in that stately progression.

The serious point at the core of such a preposterous conceit is that the Irish playwright today—or certainly the Northern Irish playwright—has to invent the theatre all over again, and conjure out of thin air (or rather out of thick and acrid air) a place within it for himself.

I suppose—given no choice—we may be better off that way. On the whole I can rest content that neither Brecht or Stanislavski were Irish. Inheritances of that kind might oppress more than they would sustain. At the same time I do firmly believe that the theatre in Ireland will continue to languish in its pragmatic, insular, stagnating condition until its practitioners develop some vital aesthetic rationale for what they're doing.

Let me suggest a possible starting-point. The international expectations from an Irish playwright remain constant—witty and extravagant language, shiftless but funny characters, pathos and hilarity intermingled. These are undeniably recurrent and distinctive features of Irish dramaturgy.

But why do they recur? What cultural force underlies these qualities which makes them virtually standard equipment for an Irish dramatist of whatever artistic persuasion?

The tenacious archaism of Irish culture has been noted elsewhere. It seems to me very likely that Irish playwrights may have in common an unconscious impulse to express the most ancient element in playacting—the instinct for play itself. Recently I have been reading Johan Huizinga's classic study of the play instinct, *Homo Ludens*, and finding it full of reverberations.

Huizinga's main contention is, of course, that culture and civilization have their origins largely in play, which precedes and envelopes them. Alongside Man the Thinker and Man the Maker, he ranks Man the Player. He has this to say with regard to the linguistic distinction between "play" and "earnest":

> The two terms are not of equal value: play is positive, earnest negative. The significance of "earnest" is defined by and exhausted in the negation of "play"—"earnest" is simply "not playing" and nothing more. The significance of "play," on the other hand, is by no means defined or exhausted by calling it "not earnest" or "not serious." Play is a thing by itself. The play-concept as such is of a higher order than is seriousness. For seriousness seeks to exclude play, whereas play can very well include seriousness.

Reading this I am drawn at once into the very wellspring of *The Importance of Being Earnest* and *The Playboy of the Western World*. Later, writing directly about the drama, Huizinga says:

> The mental sphere from which the drama springs knows no distinction between play and seriousness. With Aeschylus the experience of the most formidable seriousness is accomplished in the form of play. With Euripides, the tone wavers between profound seriousness and frivolity. The true poet, says Socrates in Plato's Symposium, must be tragic and comic at once, and the whole of human life must be felt as a blend of tragedy and comedy.

Huizinga believes that the play-spirit began to wane in the eighteenth century and has been all but extinguished by the conditions of modern life. If this is even partly true, a quintessentially ludic theatre, celebrating and re-enacting the mystery of play, would perform a crucial function in our society. This is an idea of the theatre which I myself find highly congenial. Theatre to me is amongst the most civilised and subtle of the public games that we play. The audience is a corporate player, who has licensed the playwright and actors to counterfeit reality. This licit counterfeiting is consciously entered into by both parties: an alert and responsive audience, which has freely chosen to play, is essential to the game, as essential as a high degree of craft and skill on the stage, otherwise the occasion may lapse into mere earnestness or attitudinising, and the alchemy of pleasure and enlightenment be lost.

When the game is well played the audience will be transported—but it has to be a transport of the head along with the heart. This is the other half of my programme. Let us have plays that confront the central issues of Western society, rather than those peculiar only to Crossmaglen or Connemara or Rathfarnham. These sets of issues are not, needless to say, mutually exclusive.

In this respect the precedent set by Yeats and Joyce is invaluable. They have taught us how to deal with Ireland as a manageable microcosm of the whole Western culture. The world has responded in kind.

Mention of Joyce calls Beckett to mind, and recalls Tyrone Guthrie. I am not sanguine about the likelihood of the Irish theatre responding to my strictures. I do not anticipate the theatre foyers of Dublin, Cork, Derry and Belfast suddenly filling up with budding Artauds and Grotowskis, nor with Joseph Papps and Joan Littlewoods. Even the maverick playwrights that I know mostly live and work abroad. And maybe that's as it ought to be. The nation's most authentic artistic gift may in fact be the famous genius for exile. I suspect that it is; however great the distance travelled, we never seem able to get too far from home. I started to write these ruminations on a train leaving Toronto. It was a dull wet evening, and the blasted fields on the edge of the city were waterlogged and empty. Watching this soggy landscape drift by, I caught my mind saying—this looks so forlorn and mournful and deserted, it could almost be Ireland. And so I suppose it was, in a sense.

Canadian Journal of Irish Studies 7.1 (June 1981).

Me and Jim

Yeats and Joyce, their chthonic majesties. A harmless parlour game might be to divide subsequent Irish writers between the pair of them, Yeatsians and Joyceans, the apostolic and the apostatic successions. It could maybe work, after a fashion, if less attention were paid to literary criteria than to the hazier questions of temperament, the sense of kinship, the frame of mind, the stance adopted towards the native sod.

My own mind was framed by an urban neighbourhood, a working-class family struggle towards petit-bourgeois values, a recoil from home and church and country, an appetite for exile. Scarcely surprising I should declare for Jim.

He's looking down at me now from the wall above the piano, wondering will I loan him five shillings. But I'm not doing badly by him in the matter of tribute. I've just finished a television film called *Iris In The Traffic, Ruby In The Rain,* which is a condensed female variant on the Dedalus-Bloom odyssey; I even have the rapprochement between Iris and Ruby occurring in the house of a neighbour called Joyce. Meanwhile, I'm trying to sell the idea of a television postscript to *Ulysses,* featuring the trip to Belfast by Molly Bloom and Blazes Boylan for their concert tour. Its working title is *Juanita* (or, *The Rose of Castile*) since the intention is to parody the Don Juan legend, and to end up onstage at the Ulster Hall with Blazes Boylan's trousers catching fire. Devotion can go no further, though there's a tiny motive of revenge as well for those invariably unpleasant portraits of Northerners in the Joyce canon, the likes of Mr Alleyne in "Counterparts," MacAlister of the oblong skull in *A Portrait*, the headmaster Deasy in *Ulysses.*

I was conceived shortly after Joyce died, and grew up in a Protestant Unionist family in East Belfast, and am chiefly employed in the writing of plays for stage, screen and radio. You might well ask, on any or all of these counts, what business I have affecting such a familiar tone towards James Augustine Joyce. The very fact of being at so many removes is a help, no doubt; a Dublin novelist of the forties, say, might conceivably have felt a trifle less insouciant, unless of course he happened to be Brian O'Nolan. But on the other hand, no writer in Ireland, of whatever hue or cry, can think of Joyce as less than a contemporary. Most of what is currently being written, by comparison with the work of his greatness, seems hopelessly dated. His values with regard to sex, art, nationalism, religion and much else of substance continue to be well in advance of most of the populace.

What else? In respect of drama, he offers the utmost encouragement. Stephen's theory of the aesthetic in *A Portrait* designates drama (very properly) as the highest of literary forms, because "...The aesthetic image in the dramatic form is life purified in and reprojected from the human imagination. The mystery of aesthetic like that of material creation is accomplished. The artist, like the God of the creation, remains within or behind or beyond or above his handiwork, invisible, refined out of existence, indifferent, paring his fingernails." Having formulated this, Joyce proceeded to write a drama entitled *Exiles*, in which he remained underneath, in front of, entangled up in and generally all over his handiwork, all too visible, biting his fingernails, just like any other autobiographical novelist out of his element. In addition, having been struck so forcibly as a student by Ibsen's magisterial moral vision, he possibly overlooked the coarser strains of the crafty old showman's ironical humour and melodramatic plot mechanics, the oily theatrical engine underneath the pristine dramatic fuselage. At any rate, *Exiles*, for all its fastidious styling, never really begins to take flight.

Which is of course immensely cheering for those of us in the business.

The playwright's gift or sentence is to function as a medium half-hidden in the darkness, subject to possession by the ghosts of other voices, often truer than his own. But Joyce had the very different gifts and instincts of a mimic, a solo act with star billing, out in the big spotlight. That of course was the essential difference between himself and Beckett, a man possessed by voices if ever there was one. The unique form of lyric nightmare-comedy which Beckett perfected has left its mark on the work of most playwrights who have started work since the premiere of *Waiting for Godot,* my own included. But this is a different issue to the one in hand. In terms of a profane sainthood, Joyce was a missionary and Beckett a monk: the one storming around Europe acquiring disciples and enemies, the other solitary in the anchorite's cell of his own consciousness. You can talk back to Joyce.

I knew from an early age that writing would not merely be a passion, that I would be making a life sentence out of it. The later experience of reading *Dubliners, A Portrait, Ulysses,* and Ellmann's *James Joyce* was a form of confirmation. There was so much that was familiar. In the tenacity of his emotional ties with Dublin, the possessive love mingling with the obsessive execration, the struggle over the years to annexe the place to the realm of his own imagination, I saw mirrored my own whole tangled involvement with Belfast. In his inexhaustible fascination with the idiosyncrasies of human character, I saw my own chief delight and preoccupation. In his waging of art as a battle towards an ultimate affirmation of that character, I saw my own highest aspiration. And it all warmed the cuckolds of my self-absorbed young heart.

But above all, in the decent generosity of his vision, its inclusiveness, I recognised a sane voice in the asylum. The Irelands North and South have never been less inclusive than they are at this moment. Never so many blind factions drunk with their own absolutism. And what does a writer have to offer by way of opposition? Only an imaginative struggle to enfold human diversity and then to celebrate its wholeness in art. The act of imagination may not forestall the act of slaughter, but at least it bears witness to an alternative way of carrying on in the field of human relations. And if that was good enough for Jim, then it's good enough for me.

Irish University Review 12.1 (Spring 1982).

Signposts

This year's Dublin Theatre Festival holds special significance for me. It constitutes the tenth anniversary of my professional debut in the theatre. For it was in the 1975 Festival that I finally made my first serious move into the game. I was thirty-three years old and I had fooled around long enough, trying out and discarding a succession of roles—poet, academic, broadcaster and rock music critic amongst others. Writing was my vocation. I was living through a war in my hometown, there was no time to be lost. I had a vision of life urgently demanding an audience. So I wrote a play entitled *Spokesong, or the Common Wheel*, and it opened in the second week of the Festival in the John Player Theatre on the South Circular Road.

The omens for it were not propitious, in spite of its billing— "A World Theatre Production of a World Premiere." The reality was that there were twelve other shows in the Festival, and that we were no. 13 in the batting order. But at the time it seemed a miracle to have got into the game at all.

I had written one other proper stage play, prior to *Spokesong*, in 1967. It was called *Deirdre Porter*, and I had submitted it to the Lyric which was the only viable theatre for new plays in Northern Ireland. There was no response whatsoever for two years. Then a production was unexpectedly announced. Just as discussions about casting, design and rewrites began, one of those periodic palace revolutions occurred, and the project was never heard of again—nor was the script.

At the time I was astounded by all this; I was only twenty-five. I have of course long since grown used to the neurotic, self-enraptured shambles which characterises theatre regimes the world over. Theatre people subsist on a diet of crisis. Every production is a mega-crisis, swelling up out of all the tributary crises along the way—casting, design, rehearsals, opening, reviews. The company itself, its finances, its very building, all these are permanently on the brink of armageddon.

If good work actually emerges in the teeth of all that—as it very occasionally does—then the writer, however battered and bemused, can just about cope with it. Such was not the case with the Lyric Theatre at the time. The work it was doing was execrable, and continued to be so till some years later.

From the moment (in 1974) when I conceived *Spokesong*, I realised that its only hope resided in being presented in the right way—which meant an independent production. I resolved to set this up in Belfast and then take the show to the Edinburgh Fringe Festival.

Nine months of lunacy ensued.

I began well by recruiting Michael Heffernan as the project's mentor and director. Michael was the BBC Radio Drama producer at the time, and had just done an exciting production of my radio play, *The Iceberg*. As soon as I had drafted the first act of *Spokesong*, I read it aloud to him, and he immediately committed himself to the enterprise and started lobbying the Arts Council for a grant towards the production. Then I wrote the second act, and he read that, and pretty much advised me to tear it up and try again. So I did, and indeed continued to do so, never entirely abandoning the effort till a further four years had elapsed.

But in the meantime we had a play of sorts, we had both conviction *and* a passionate intensity, and we had between us a sound body of radio work in drama, complete with glowing press notices. So on January 28th, 1975, we made our initial application for subsidy to the Arts Council of Northern Ireland.

The first setback was that they could not consider work which was intended for presentation outside the Province. Fine, no sweat. If they would enable us to mount the show in Belfast, we would raise funds from other sources to take it to

Edinburgh. In February I actually went over there and confidently booked a venue; I was hugely tempted by a moped showroom called Better Bikes which was run by a former member of the 7:84 Company, but settled in the end for a conventional (but legally viable) church hall.

A word about the play. I was possessed then, as I am now, with the challenge of forging a unifying dramatic metaphor for the Northern Irish human condition. I take it as given that the tribal, sectarian malevolence in this society is the deepest, most enduring and least tractable evil in our inheritance: not the border, nor the discrimination, nor the corruption, nor any of the other repellent *symptoms*. In my view, sectarian exclusiveness is the First Cause, for our purposes—however much you may care to argue about its historical origins. All the rest is predicated on it.

I see no point in writing a plea for unity between prods and taigs. What use has piety been? I can only see a point in actually embodying that unity, practising that inclusiveness, in an artistic image; creating it as an act of the imagination, postulating it before an audience. There have been political visionaries in our shared but fractured tradition who have like the grandparents in *Spokesong* briefly sustained such an image in the past—Henry Joy McCracken being one. For a playwright, the task carries a rather smaller burden of risk—we aren't often hung as a consequence of it (although like Sam Thompson, we may well work ourselves into a premature grave)—nor are we required to kill those who take issue with us, however great the temptation in particular cases. Nevertheless, the responsibility is a grave one.

In *Spokesong*, I adopted a unifying image precisely on the basis of its incongruity: a decrepit bicycle shop. One of my strategies was to try to write a play about violence which would ambush the audience with pleasure, and there are few subjects more pleasurable than the history of the bicycle. Then again, it is an aspect of social history which runs (I can put it in no other way) in tandem with the political history of the

Unionist/Nationalist ideological divide, in an uncanny and provocative fashion. The period from Dunlop's 1888 invention of the pneumatic tyre in Belfast, to the ecology movement bike-revival of the early nineteen seventies, encompasses the end of Parnellism, Randolph Churchill and the Orange Card, the Home Rule Bills, the Great War, Partition, and so on, right up to Bloody Sunday and Bloody Friday.

So I was enabled to have a family shop (partly inspired by the erstwhile Stones bike shop in Cromac Square) founded by a grandfather, Francis Stock, who had wooed and won the flamboyant Kitty Carberry. They had been Victorian idealists of wildly conflicting hues—she a Maud-Gonne-style Nationalist, he an Empire Loyalist. The only bond between them was a passionate love of the bicycle, which is a form of love for humanity itself. But their unquiet ghosts still haunt the shop in 1973, when it is jointly owned by their grandson Frank Stock, the play's protagonist, a good-natured man, and his brother Julian, an implacably bitter one. Frank falls for a customer, a teacher called Daisy Bell, who is a hard-headed pragmatist with a U.D.A. commander for a father. Julian competes with Frank for Daisy's favours and for control of the shop's destiny. The shop is meanwhile threatened from without by both bombs and by re-development.

I felt that I had at long last found a way of embracing the whole city, my city, in this play. I was desperate for it to be seen first by a Belfast audience.

So I set about some serious hustling. I roped in Brian Garrett, solicitor and theatre enthusiast, who drew up an appeal for funds endorsed by three Belfast luminaries from contrasting fields of achievement—the athlete Mary Peters, the shipyard trades unionist Sandy Scott, and the actor James Ellis. The appeal went first to the City Council and the Dunlop Tyre Company, and then to a list of twenty commercial institutions, requesting programme sponsorship.

Meanwhile, Michael Heffernan and I had adopted a corporate identity, Ixion Productions, complete with headed notepaper, and had formed the nucleus of a company. Stephen Rea was to play Frank. I had known him since Queen's University days, he had played the leading role in *The Iceberg*, and he was very much the rising star in London theatre, but extremely keen, even then, to do serious work back home again. Another London exile, Allan McClelland, signed on to play Francis, the grandfather. Michael Poynor applied himself to the costing of the whole enterprise. We were on our way.

In March I talked to Hibby Wilmot about presenting a show in the Arts Theatre, and in April I spent a spirituous evening with Michael Barnes, director of the Queen's Festival, who had read the play and was full of praise for it. In both cases the enthusiasm was tempered by the only qualification: the Arts Council money would have to pay for the production. There would be no additional funds.

I forget now how much we had asked for. I think it was around £2,000. At any rate, the Arts Council's Drama Officer, Frank Murphy, was assuring us at the end of April that we were almost certain to get it. The committee had met on the 22nd, and was very favourably disposed. From that point on, the whole thing fell to pieces.

Garrett's appeal, ignored altogether in some cases, politely fobbed off in others, ended up with just one positive response— an offer of £75 from British Rail. As an ironist, I felt very keenly the poetic aptness of this donor, whose services I would later engage to take a one-way journey out … but that's another story, involving subsequent Arts Council rejection. In this instance it was on May 20th that we learnt from Frank Murphy that the Arts Council had received a smaller government subvention than they had anticipated and that we wouldn't be receiving a penny from them.

I kept right on hustling, but it was clearly curtains so far as Belfast was concerned. I even remember at one point talking wildly to James Ford Smith about putting the play on in the Ulster Museum. On May 22nd I travelled to Nottingham, where Heffernan was convalescing from a serious operation, for a conference with him, Stephen Rea and Allan McClelland. It was effectively the end of Ixion Productions.

Dublin was clearly the next place to turn, and Michael proposed an approach to Godfrey Quigley, who with Donal Donnelly ran the aforementioned World Theatre Company, more or less from the glove compartment of Godfey's car. They in turn offered a production to the Dublin Theatre Festival, and by July 22nd a deal was done. We were scheduled for the Project Theatre, but the administration there had a falling-out with Brendan Smith, the Festival Director, and we were consigned to the John Player.

This is a venue unique in Ireland, and possibly the world. It is a constituent part of the Player-Wills cigarette factory, and is consequently permeated with the smell of tobacco whilst being entirely devoid of a liquor licence. It also has a flat end-stage. Many of the entrances and exits in *Spokesong* have to be accomplished on bicycles. To recap, the omens were not propitious.

They became less and less so as we came to grips with the thin little shoestring of a budget we had been given. For instance, there was no provision whatever for a set designer. No knowing any designers, much less one who would work for nothing, I asked my Belfast architect friend, John Gilbert—a fellow-communard in our house in Rugby Road—to do us a set. He had no previous theatre experience of any kind, but he ended up doing a handsome job, and posters to match, and bringing them all down to Dublin in his car, along with some borrowed spotlights, and other friends from the house to help build and paint the set … it was a case of let's do the show right here—and then let's take it right down there.

We were lucky to end up with a remarkably strong cast all told, including Raymond Hardie as Frank, Barry McGovern as Julian, Ruth Hegarty as Daisy and Maire ni Ghráinne as Kitty. I was myself to be found at various times supervising costume hire, fetching accessories from the Irish Raleigh factory, and painting the bicycle ramp we had built, from the side aisle up on to the stage, an hour before the first-night audience was due to appear.

The opening night was like nothing before or since. My wife and I went off to the flat we had borrowed to clean up and change for the big event, only for the front door key to snap off in the lock as we tried to get in. We had to ask near-strangers close by if we could come in and use their bathroom for a few minutes. Back at the theatre, I spent a brief, anguished spell watching the play, and then retired to my whiskey bottle in the car; only to be fetched back during the intermission in order to be presented to the Irish President.

What happened later was considerably more astonishing. The Dublin critics were mostly enthusiastic but the London ones were electrifying. The play was very soon optioned by the Royal Court Theatre, and then bought by the National Theatre of Belgium. In the event, it was at the King's Head Theatre that it opened in September 1976—and instantly created a sensation, running there for six months before transferring briefly to the West End. By November I was sitting in the Théâtre National in Brussels, filled with incredulity at the spectacle of Frank chatting up Daisy in elegant French. In February 1977, I was sitting in the Savoy Hotel in London, listening to Peter Ustinov announcing that I had won the *Evening Standard* Drama Award for Most Promising Playwright of the year, and then stepping up to receive the proverbial statuette from Glenda Jackson, my ears still blocked up from flying in on the Belfast shuttle, which increased the sense of unreality.

After that, the play left home and started living its own life, mostly without me. Programmes and reviews came in from all over—the Royal Theatre in Copenhagen, various places in Finland and Sweden and Norway. For a prolonged spell, it was really big in Holland. Then it was done in Australia, and then in New Zealand, and then in Canada.

And finally, the U.S.A. The Long Wharf Theatre in New Haven premiered it in 1978, and the New York critics burst into song. The following year, we actually opened on Broadway, and I was actually given an opening-night party in Sardi's, sitting in a drunken heap of nerves and hilarity.

So you will understand if I wish *Spokesong* a very happy tenth birthday and many happy returns.

It did at length reach Belfast, Northern Ireland, in the twelfth and final week of an Irish Theatre Company tour out of Dublin in 1978, a production which I missed, but which seemed to provoke very little excitement around town.

Maybe some company will eventually accord it a Northern Irish premiere, when the time seems ripe again. Or maybe not. Personally, I plan to leave well alone.

Theatre Ireland 11 (Autumn 1985).

Introduction to *Lost Belongings*

Most television drama projects have knocked around for a while before they finally reach the viewer—but probably for not quite so long as was the case with *Lost Belongings*. The bones of the Deirdre Connell story are well over a thousand years old, just for a start; though the specific character herself originated in more recent times, twenty years ago, when I made a first maladroit attempt to write a full-blown stage play dealing with her fate.

Moving into the era of recorded history, I have dug out of the box file a letter to a producer friend, dated January 1981, which goes as follows:

> I'm mulling over the feasibility of a trilogy of films set in Ulster during the last fourteen years. What has happened is that various and sundry ideas have suddenly grouped themselves together in my mind. The three films have different characters, different milieus and tones of voice, but they all deal with individuals whose lives are affected by the large events in the midst of which they're trying to live. And taken together, they should present a composite picture of sorts, a summation of the Northern Irish seventies. The sort of antecedent I have in mind is the Wajda trilogy about wartime Poland...

There follows a summary of the three plot-lines: the first being the growing up of Alec Ferguson and Craig Connell, entitled *Buck Alec*, the second being the Gretchen Reilly/Simon Hunt/McBraill/Riddel thriller which would become *The American Friend*, and the third the Lenny Harrigan story as told in *Lenny Leaps In*.

This treatment was unsuccessfully trawled around the television companies by a couple of different freelance producers and directors in the course of the next two years. In the meantime, a conjunction began to form in my mind between these three narratives and the timeless Deirdre tragedy to which I still longed to do some kind of justice.

The marriage between them was consummated in the autumn of 1982, when yet another producer, at the BBC, invited me to submit a scheme for a six-part series. I simply added to the trilogy of existing stories a fourth tale which gave a fuller account of Hugh McBraill, and then placed them all within the embrace of Deirdre's rise and fall.

The BBC got as far as commissioning the script of the first film, which was written in the Spring of 1983 […] However, after thirteen months of careful deliberation, they decided not to proceed with the series, which then went back into limbo for a bit. […]

My original treatment for the six-film format has this to say about creating a latter day version of the Deirdre myth:

> Although a modern audience would be unaware of the source, I'm convinced that stories as timeless as this one contain a universal resonance, which lends them infinitely more value than a merely anecdotal narrative. A well-worn sentiment, rather pompously expressed; but I still go along with it.

When I finally got the chance to write films number 2-6 (at the behest of David Elstein at Primetime Television who had been shown the existing material by my indefatigable agent, Marc Berlin), it was the end of 1984. But I decided to retain 1980 as the year in which the immediate events of the story take place. My reasoning was subjective.

These scripts are not autobiographical; they actually feel a touch more personal than that. I had been a resident of Belfast, my native city, up until 1978. Having lived there for a total of thirty-one years, I feel entitled to go on writing about it indefinitely. However, the fabric of time and place and incident is very intricate and specific in these stories, so that each additional year away felt like another bandage wound around my writing hand. I wasn't living there, for example, when the ten Maze hunger strikers died in 1981. I wasn't living there when the Anglo-Irish Agreement was signed at Hillsborough in 1985. I would not have felt comfortable trying to express how events such as those impinged directly on the lives of these particular characters.

At any rate, drama needs some measure of distance to achieve any kind of coherence. If the distance can't be emotional, then it has to be historical.

The document known in film and television producers' office as a "treatment" is a logical absurdity. It is a summary of and an evocation of and a commentary upon something which is entirely without existence: namely, a script. But until they feel secure with your treatment, they won't engage you to write your script.

If I seem to keep quoting from the various *Lost Belongings* treatments, it is only because I am amazed by their temerity: which arises, of course, from desperation. So desperate are you to sell a producer on the unwritten script that you're driven to ever wilder shores of heady rhetoric. You'll promise them anything.

In the final treatment for this series, I started out with the Big Picture:

> There is by now a widespread feeling throughout Britain that Northern Ireland is the black hole of British politics, into which normal principles, issues and panaceas disappear without trace. Because the inter-communal conflict has so many inter-locking elements—nationalist, religious, colonial, ethnic, class, economic—the situation presents a seemingly intractable challenge to democratic solutions. The one certainty is that it won't go away.

There follows a passage of political attitudinising. It seems to me that a writer's personal politics are actually neither here nor

[112]

there: it's only the politics embodied in and expressed through the work that will matter; and the two are often interestingly at odds, for the imagination dredges far deeper than opinions or even convictions. Furthermore, the fruits of the imagination are earned through long and arduous labour, and I see no point in selling it short with an easy recitation of banal slogans, however sincerely meant. Or at any rate that's the theory, and the next bit of the treatment seeks to engage with it:

> If I merely wanted to expound such views, I would be a polemicist or a political journalist rather than a playwright. As a playwright, my overriding concern is to keep faith with the individual lives and aspirations of all my characters, and yet do equal justice to the big public events and historical forces which have been crucial in shaping their destinies. In this way I hope to throw a little light into the black hole, to enable an audience to perceive the thing in personal and human and entertaining terms rather than as a baffling muddle of irreconcilable abstractions.

Quite apart from the embarrassing misuse of the black-hole metaphor, these are the kind of pieties to which an Irishman feels driven in order to persuade an English company (the only kind likely to make you an offer) to invest over three million pounds in his wildest dreams.

From the vantage point of the completed series, I can freely own up that the audience with which I was first and foremost concerned, then as now, and as in everything else I have ever written, was my own people, the people of Northern Ireland, Ulster, the Six counties, Lilliput, a place so fundamentally factional that it can't even agree on a name for itself. And also that my intentions were not all so reassuring. Tragedy is endemic to the human condition, which is why it forms the stuff of myth, death is certain and universal, Ireland has never been at one, all well and good or sick and bad; but if classical tragedy is intended to purge its audience of pity and terror, this mongrel tragedy of the death of Deirdre Connell aims to provoke shame and rage, that she should be let die, like a hounded animal, outside the locked door of Ulster Christianity.

Northern Ireland is the conscience as well as the cockpit of Thatcher's Monarchy and Haughey's Republic, and it's a bad conscience in both cases, and a remorselessly bloody cockpit and therefore left off the agenda as comprehensively as possible.

How many more times must the death of Deirdre Connell be re-enacted?

In the beginning was the Word—the treatment first, and then the scripts—and a long way after that, the Action—budgeting, casting, directing, designing, lighting, shooting, editing, dubbing. Finally, the Screening.

By which time, in the normal course of film-making, the Word has long since been forgotten, left standing at the starting-post. But the case of *Lost Belongings* was very different from the norm, […] the Word was treated with great respect throughout the Action, by all and sundry. In the argot of the trade, we were all making the same movie; a much rarer state of affairs than it may sound. The fascination of film is its volatility, its flux, the multifarious elements which constantly qualify and alter one another—and the script, far from being Holy Writ, is one of those elements, shifting and changing in response to the others. You might assume that the writer is owed a place on the team, as shifter and changer in his own department; unless you happen to be a producer or director, in which case you probably assume no such thing. But on this (for me) happy occasion all the cuts, transpositions, rewrites and extra bits which were called for throughout the Action were indeed entrusted to the writer, and duly supplied, in buses, planes, hotel bars, abandoned churches, disused warehouses, derelict distilleries, and even from time to time in my own study. […]

Once television films are made, they have to be cut down to size—in this case to what is known as "the ITV Hour," which can never be longer than fifty-one and a half minutes and is not generally shorter than forty-nine and a half (kindly reflect upon the fact that this is English television with which we are dealing and not Irish). [...]

The Word would never have got this far if the project had not been so fortunate in the friends which it eventually made: principally David Elstein who commissioned the films, Barry Hanson who produced them, Tony Bicât who directed them, and John Hambley and colleagues at Euston Films and Channel 4 who ended up making them. I am indebted to these, as to all my other collaborators—the cast, and the standing army behind the scenes without whose multifarious skills the Word cannot be made flesh.

This is a slightly edited version of the introduction Parker wrote for the Euston Films/Thames Television edition of the script of *Lost Belongings*. The full text is published with the screenplay in *Stewart Parker Television Plays* (2008). The first episode of *Lost Belongings* was aired on 7th April 1987 by ITV.

Foreword to *Plays: 2*

I. Ancestral voices prophesy and bicker, and the ghosts of your own time and birthplace wrestle and dance, in any play you choose to write—but most obviously when it actually is a history play.

The three history plays in this volume were conceived and written, in consecutive order, between 1983 and 1987, as a common enterprise. Trilogy, however, may be too strong a word for them. Triptych has a more pleasing ring: three self-contained groups of figures, from the eighteenth, nineteenth and twentieth centuries respectively, hinged together in a continuing comedy of terrors.

The ancestral wraiths at my own elbow are (amongst other things) Scots-Irish, Northern English, immigrant Huguenot ... in short the usual Belfast mongrel crew, who have contrived between them to entangle me in the whole Irish-British cat's cradle and thus to bequeath to me a subject for drama which is comprised of multiplying dualities: two islands (the "British Isles"), two Irelands, two Ulsters, two men fighting over a field.

II. Plays and ghosts have a lot in common. The energy which flows from some intense moment of conflict in a particular time and place seems to activate them both. Plays intend to achieve resolution, however, whilst ghosts appear to be stuck fast in the quest for vengeance. Ghosts are uncompleted souls; witness the Phantom Bride in *Northern Star,* handing on to the Phantom Fiddler in *Heavenly Bodies,* and he in turn to *Pentecost's* Lily Matthews—in whom the cycle of retribution is in fact finally laid to rest, in the only way I can foresee as having any possible meaning.

III. So far as the "real" characters are concerned, they have been drawn from the marginalia of the historical record rather than its main plot. Henry Joy McCracken was a minor figure in the '98 Rising in Ireland; not enough is known about him. Dion Boucicault was unarguably a major force in the Victorian theatre, but then that is a period of drama which is in itself considered marginal nowadays; rather more than enough is known about him. McCracken's mistress, Mary Bodle, is so obscure that her name might well have been Boall. Boucicault's Mephistophelean sparring partner, Johnny Patterson, survives precariously as a name on fading sheet-music covers. He did certainly write "The Garden Where the Praties Grow," as well as "The Hat My Father Wore" (which, suitably altered, was to be taken over as the favourite anthem of Orangeism) ... and also, incidentally, "The Stone Outside Dan Murphy's Door," a record of which was the most cherished offering on my grandfather Jimmy Lynas's old wind-up gramophone. Harold Wilson, whose recorded voice is briefly heard in the third play, was Prime Minister of the United Kingdom of Great Britain and Northern Ireland in the years 1964-70 and 1974-76.

IV. The first play employs pastiche as a strategy, and the second one a kind of collage; the third play is written in a form of heightened realism. This seemed most appropriate for my own generation, finally making its own scruffy way onto the stage of history and from thence into the future tense, in this climactic piece.

(1989)*

---

* The Methuen Drama *Plays: 2* includes the plays *Northern Star*, *Heavenly Bodies* and *Pentecost*. Parker's foreword is incorrectly dated 1989; it should be 1988.

Postscript

Stewart Parker's drama is a quirky yet compelling blend of the comic and the intellectual. The fusion of ideas and fun in the seven plays published by Methuen Drama has won many admirers, and this body of work alone establishes Parker as an important writer. Yet as time has passed the drama stands increasingly detached from his other writing. The whole picture of Parker's life-work is already a faded one. Yes, we have the main figures (the stage plays) but the other elements that might complete or enhance the composition are becoming faint and obscure. So in a sense this collection is an act of restoration as well as of celebration; by assembling scattered and archive-bound work we hope a richer understanding of Parker's accomplishments will emerge.

The essays, radio script, newspaper articles and lecture gathered here complement and illuminate the dramatic work currently in print. Some of this material is familiar (at least to the initiated)—*Dramatis Personae*, the Foreword to *Plays: 2*—while the remainder has been largely unavailable to all but the most diligent researchers.

The dominant impression derived from these pieces is a powerful sense of interconnectedness, nothing goes to waste. Parker returns to the formative experiences of his youth and refines his ideas concerning the vital, if troubled, relations of theatre and politics, art and life. This is undoubtedly most fully articulated in the *Dramatis Personae* lecture, yet is threaded through all of the pieces here. The politics of poverty and under-privilege that underpin the American prison system observed in "School for Revolution" find subtle counterpoint in Parker's work on Sam Thompson and the latter's dramatisation of Belfast's working class life. His impatience with the dearth of ideas and the self-indulgence of American experimental theatre in the sixties—"It's a Bad Scene, Mrs Worthington"—and a commitment to intelligent *and* playful writing is distilled in "State of Play" and, finally, decanted in *Dramatis Personae*.

This volume emerged amidst a confluence of projects involving the work of Stewart Parker and is one of a number of publications aiming to celebrate Parker's achievements on the twentieth anniversary of his death. Parker's *High Pop* column, which he wrote for *The Irish Times*, is published by Lagan Press (Belfast) in a single volume edited by Gerald Dawe and Maria Johnston. *Plays for Radio and Stage* edited by Mark Phelan is also published by Lagan Press, while *Television Plays* edited by Clare Wallace is the companion piece to this volume and is published by Litteraria Pragensia.

Clare Wallace